HARD A TAB NAB

HARD A TAB NAB

Master Mariner J. R. de L. Inniss

ARTHUR H. STOCKWELL LTD
Torrs Park   Ilfracombe   Devon
Established 1898
www.ahstockwell.co.uk

ISBN 978-0-7223-4135-3
Printed in Great Britain by
Arthur H. Stockwell Ltd
Torrs Park   Ilfracombe
Devon

CONTENTS

PREFACE

I hope these stories of the halcyon days of British shipping will bring back memories to some and also be somewhat of an historical record to others who still have an interest in the sea and our once proud merchant marine.

The period I have written about is from 1950 to the mid 1990s. Some of the ships I served on were grim old bangers, with diabolical food; others were beautiful-looking vessels with fine lines, flared bows, and strong scantlings.

On the cargo ships in particular, loading and discharging the varied amounts of cargo was an art form in itself.

Down in the engine room, officers worked quite often in humid conditions with high temperatures. Many of the engines were of the heavy steam reciprocating type, but they had a beauty of their own when working. Other ships had large marine diesel engines, some with two engines side by side driving two propellers. An engineer's recurrent nightmare on these ships was a fire in the funnel uptake. Known as scavenge fires, they were very difficult to put out.

All the officers were qualified to a very high standard. The pass mark for deck and engineer written examinations was 70%. A very rigid oral examination followed.

The voyages were long – usually in excess of six months. Conditions on board were spartan; there was no air conditioning; and only the captain and chief engineer were allowed to take their wives with them.

Crews were often British nationals, but a very large proportion of the ships carried Asian crews, known as Lascars. Most of these men came from India, Pakistan and Bangladesh. Chinese were quite often carried on ships dependent on the trade to the Far East.

Working hours for all hands were long. A ten-hour day at sea was the norm – and even longer in port – but there were compensations. The ships spent long periods in most ports of the world, so there was an opportunity to see distant countries at first hand.

All this changed with the advent of air travel (which gradually made all the world look the same), and of course the container ships and the supertankers. It was almost gone by 1980, there then being just over 300 registered British ships. I was fortunate to have sailed on the best of them.

I enjoyed a marvellous life at sea, and I hope you will enjoy the tales in this book.

Master Mariner J. R. de L. Inniss, Ashwater, Devon.

BOY SEAMAN ON THE WHEEL

I was fourteen years of age when I first went to sea. From the time I was taken aboard an LST (landing ship tank) off Falmouth in 1945, I was hooked. I loved everything, from the smell of oil and paint below decks to the stories the crew told me of life on the high seas and in foreign places.

Joining the Sea Cadets in Bideford, I must have been one of the last to march along Bideford Quay with a rifle and fixed bayonet. We operated from a retired MTB (motor torpedo boat) tied up alongside in the river, and gradually shipboard life became ingrained in us. We marched, and we did rifle drill. The Oerlikon 20-mm gun was stripped down and put back together again, over and over again, until we could do it blindfold. It was a good thing there was no ammunition; otherwise I am sure someone would have fired it.

In November 1954 I volunteered to go on HMS *Illustrious* for a two-week voyage. Another lad, a fisherman's son from Appledore, came with me. My mother was in a right panic over the idea, but Father said, "Let him go. It will do him good, one way or another."

So off we went by train from Exeter to Portsmouth. The *Illustrious* looked massive from the quayside. She was berthed alongside HMS *Victory*, and the two ships really brought home to me the power of the Royal Navy.

We boys were berthed in a large area in the forepart of the

ship, directly under the flight deck. Hammocks were issued and we were told how to rig them and stow them during the daytime. There were almost forty young men from all over the country, so the mess deck was pretty crowded. All the orders on board were announced by the bosun's pipe calls, or a bugle, and they went on virtually all day from 'rise and shine' to 'lights out'.

The navy marched us about everywhere, and a programme of training was laid out. A most serious lecture was given to us all in the officers' mess by the ship's padre about some of the nasty things we might see during our time on board – including aircraft crashing, which was quite common, apparently.

The ship sailed, and she went out into the Channel to 'fly on' aircraft. This was most exciting. The planes were fixed-wing Avengers, and some jets called Sea Hawks. Nobody crashed. Then, after a stop off the Isle of Wight, we went out into the Atlantic and the Irish Sea, flying aircraft on and off and test-firing the ship's guns.

We lads were shown the engine room, entry to which was through an air lock. It was not very pleasant. The ladder down was clouded with steam, and it was very hot. We were fourteen-year-old boys, and it took a lot of nerve to go below.

I was in the fo'c's'le party when the ship anchored off Cowes. A large burly chief petty officer told us, "That is the port anchor; that is the starboard anchor; and that one lashed up to the bulkhead is the spare or bower anchor." To me it sounded like 'barr anchor'. This was to be my downfall later on in the cruise.

I cleaned masses of brass down on the quarterdeck, with the sea rushing past a few feet away. This area was reserved for the senior officers to take their daily walks. I got in conversation with one who had four stripes on his shoulders. We got on fine until an even more senior officer appeared and was most upset that this lowly seaman was chatting to the Captain.

One morning my Appledore pal and I were taken right down into the bowels of the ship, nine decks down, to the 'action stations' steering position. Access was through a small manhole, and once we were inside this was shut watertight, and a marine guard was placed outside to ensure nobody panicked and left.

Without going into the mechanics of it, there were three different steering systems in this small place, and it must have been a frightening part of the ship to be in when the ship was being bombed in the Mediterranean by German and Italian aircraft during the war.

We were shown how to steer, and after a while I was allowed to steer the ship on my own. Aircraft were being flown on and off, but down there we had no knowledge of that. I thought I was doing all right until over the Tannoy a voice from the bridge demanded, "Who is on the wheel? Steer small. The ship's all over the place."

"Boy Seaman Inniss on the wheel, sir," I stammered.

The senior quartermaster then got a rocket and my brief stint on the wheel was over.

My Appledore friend had a brother who was a marine bugler on board. He operated from a small office high up on the ship's island, and we two got up there and started spending the days with him. This was absolutely fantastic fun as we could watch the planes landing and taking off and also the testing of the guns. Some of the landings were pretty hairy, and one plane crashed into the base of the island, but no harm was done to the pilot.

We spent hours up there, until one morning there was a large explosion in one of the gun turrets and all hell broke loose. The ship was sealed off, and the two of us got into serious trouble for not being where we should have been. We heard later that some men had been killed in one of the 4.5-inch gun turrets and several more were badly hurt.

Illustrious was now steaming in the Irish Sea, and we lads were given an examination to see how much we had learnt and whether we were suitable to join the Royal Navy. An officer was detailed to ask us the questions. We each had three to answer; two right was not enough to pass.

My first two questions were easy ones, then came the third: "How many anchors are on the ship and what are they called?"

"The port and starboard anchors and the barr anchor."

I thought, 'Here I go – first step on the way to being an admiral.'

"Wrong!" bawled the officer. "It's the bower anchor."

I was marked down as unsuitable for the Royal Navy.

The ship stopped again off the Isle of Wight and most of the young men went home. My friend from Appledore was sent off for fighting with some of the more undesirable elements of the lower deck. I stayed behind. I was enjoying the life.

The daily rum issue was a memorable event, with a Royal Marine guard over the barrels of rum, and the sweet, heavy smell of the coal-black rum as it was dished out. Because of my age I was not allowed any, but I signed my issue away for 'threepence on my wages'. I was not being paid, so I think someone amongst the crew had my ration.

I had now been on the ship almost three weeks and, unbeknown to me, my mother was going frantic. Apparently the navy had forgotten me. Suddenly, anchored off Bangor in Northern Ireland, I was hauled out of my hammock and told I was going home forthwith.

Ratings were not allowed to use the accommodation ladder to get into shore boats; the jackstay was their means of getting off the ship. A large wooden boom was heaved out over the ship's side with a net underneath it to catch strays. The shore boats would come in under the end of the boom, and down you would go, hanging on to a rope ladder. Finally you would fall in a heap in the bottom of the boat. Your kitbag would be thrown in after you.

It was a rough, blustery night when I went over the side. It was blowing hard and it was not easy staying on the slippery wooden boom. The boat was bouncing about under the ladder and the coxswain was yelling at me to get a move on.

The trip ashore was not pleasant either, and I was feeling

decidedly queasy by the time I got on board the ferry for Hollyhead.

The voyage across the Irish Sea was very rough, and I was very sick. The ship was full of soldiers going home on leave, and the bar was very busy. I lay down on the deck outside in the gale, not feeling very pleased with myself.

Getting home from Holyhead took ages. I had no idea where the trains took me. Eventually I arrived back at Bideford Railway Station. My father and mother met me – and the local press, as Mother had fired them up over my situation.

"How was it?" asked my old man.

"Great," replied the Boy Seaman. "Nothing to it!"

SUNSHINE ON PARADE

The icy wind swept across the parade ground. Commands rang out, and naval cadets formed line.

"Present arms!" The drill instructor's voice rasped across the sodden square.

I dropped my rifle.

"Pick it up, laddie, pick it up."

My fingers, wracked with poison under the nails from days of cleaning kit and gear, just would not function. I was marched off to the sickbay in some disgrace.

Three weeks earlier I had joined the training college straight from school. My headmaster had wished me luck as he sent me on my way. I had signed the papers removing me from national service in the army, with the catch that if I left the merchant service before I was twenty-six, into the army I would go.

I spent a day in the naval outfitters in Southampton Docks. The salesman was called Mr Noaks, and he had a permanent sniff. Shirts, dungarees, boots, caps and boiler suits were laid out in an ever increasing pile. That most important tool of every sailor, a knife with marlin spikes, all contained in a leather pouch, was dropped by Noaks on to the pile of clothing. Then came his final masterpiece: with a deprecating masterful series of sniffs I was kitted out with a blue uniform with the gold cuff buttons of a cadet, a blue battledress, and, the most important item of all, a blue mess kit. The white waistcoat had gold buttons, and the trousers had a broad blue stripe down the leg. To top it off, I was given a boat cloak with a gold neck chain. Noaks looked at my mother and gave a long sniff.

"A most essential item, madam."

Noaks looked up at the ceiling as though someone up above commanded the purchase of this last expensive piece of clothing.

And so, after packing it all away into two large trunks, which also were on the kit list, my mother drove me the few miles out of town and into the merchant navy. I was just seventeen, and I was not to finish with it until over forty years later.

My mother left me at the guardhouse and I was allocated a cabin in the starboard watch with five other young men. We were then indoctrinated in the very forbidding rules. Disobeying an order meant instant dismissal. Minor infringements meant doing overtime. There would be no walking anywhere, except in the classrooms or the dining hall; anywhere else, we had to move at the double.

Reveille would be at 0530 hours every morning, and all hands would assemble on the parade ground in running kit for the compulsory 2-mile morning run. This would be followed by a cold shower and shave and then cabin-cleaning for an inspection before breakfast. After we had all eaten, an hour was then spent learning Morse code, semaphore, all the code flags used at sea, and, most importantly, flag etiquette. There then followed divisional parade. The whole college assembled on the parade ground, and the colour guard with rifles and fixed bayonets marched into position between the two parade cannons and the flagpole. Full inspection was then carried out before the bugler blew 'stand by', and the colours were hoisted precisely at 0800 hours.

The food in this ex-naval establishment was of the highest quality, and there was plenty of it. This was owing mainly to the director's wife, who insisted the cadets had plenty of meat and vegetables, and well-cooked meals. They were certainly needed.

The rest of the day then followed with lectures on navigation, seamanship and ship stability. Meteorology was hammered into us from the beginning, along with mathematics and nautical law.

Further inspections took place before dinner in the evening, and eventually at 2130 hours 'lights out' was blown by the bugler and the cadets turned in. We slept six to a cabin with the windows open top and bottom whatever the weather outside. It was quite common to wake in the morning with frost on the top blanket.

This was the routine for the next three months.

So there I was, admitted to the sickbay, and the forbidding-looking matron took one look at me, stripped my clothes off and ordered me into a very hot bath, where I lay for at least an hour. Then she cleaned out the profusion of whitlows in my fingers and ordered me to bed for two days. She was always at odds with the hierachy of the Naval College over their treatment of cadets, and it was her policy to pull in one of them every now and then and clean them up and let them rest. I returned to the fold a few days later feeling much better and ready now for my nautical training to crack on.

We all put up with the interminable inspections and parades, and arms and close-order drills on the parade ground, but we became increasingly fit in both body and mind. My weight went from about 8 stone to 11, all solid muscle.

One aspect of our training was 'learning how to defend yourself in foreign ports'. This training was done by an ex-professional wrestler, a certain Jimmy Noice. There were very few of us who enjoyed this trial of all-in wrestling. Noice was a hard man, and failure to get fully stuck in to the lesson would mean you ended up fighting him, or trying to, which usually meant ending up with all the tendons in your arms and legs being twisted out of shape into agonizing positions. One young man told Mr Noice he would not fight like that in reality, and when asked how, the cadet flattened Jimmy with a straight

She was silenced by the Bishop.

The Admiral then piped up and said to the Skeleton, "My boy, it would be a good idea to cut across the spit inside the buoy and save time."

"'Tis against orders, sir," quavered the Skeleton.

"Bollicks!" the Bishop's mother cut in. "Nelson turned a blind eye."

Between the two of them, and the fact that the Admiral was the most senior officer on board, the Skeleton relented.

"Backwater port, up starboard," he ordered.

Putting the helm over, we shot across inside the buoy towards the College Pier.

I felt my oar touch bottom. Sunshine threw up a scoopful of shale. The skiff came to a grinding halt, fast aground. I could see the welcoming party on the pier, jumping about. Boy, were we in trouble!

The Bishop's mother said, "I can walk."

"No, you bloody well can't," I told her. "You will drown if you do."

Sunshine then shipped his oar and jumped over the side. This lightened the boat considerably. He came round to the stern and gave some mighty shoves, and off we shot, leaving Sunshine swimming in the now fast current. Somehow we got him alongside and hauled him into the stern, soaking the now chastened visiting party and sobering the Bishop's mother up somewhat.

A few minutes later we were alongside the pier and the party disappeared up the ladder. The Superintendent's head appeared, looking down at us.

"You will all report to my office immediately. Anchor the skiff and double across the parade ground." His bushy eyebrows were clamped into a fierce line.

For the serious offence of disobeying orders the Skeleton was dismissed from the college. Sunshine and I were told that our chances of promotion were seriously reduced. I didn't like the Skeleton, but I said to the Superintendent that he *was* obeying orders – the orders of a senior naval officer. But it didn't wash, and Skeleton packed his bags and left.

He was back a week later. His parents, who were paying his fees, put pressure on the college to reinstate him. I heard a few years later that he had been crushed to death by a faulty metal hatch lid on a bulk carrier he was working on.

Meanwhile the summer term continued – drills, parades, and for me one hour's drill on the parade ground for talking in the ranks. The fact that a large mosquito had been biting chunks out of my face did not wash with Billy, the parade instructor.

Drill was a most fearsome punishment, especially in hot weather. Full battledress was worn, including a rifle with fixed bayonet, and heavy boots. All precautions were taken to minimize the effects of the drilling. Sponge pads were worn under the shirt on the left shoulder, and there was even extra padding around the groin. Six of us set off at a brisk march around the parade ground, then, after about five minutes, Billy ordered, "Double time, march!" Off we went, round and round, at the same time shouldering arms, sloping arms, fixing and unfixing bayonets, and, worst of all, presenting arms. This was where the bodily protection was useful.

One lad fell out after about half an hour and was carried off to the sickbay. The rest of us continued. I refused to let the system get to me, and at last Billy ordered, "Halt and dismiss!"

We were marched back to the guardroom. I was soaked with sweat in all my clothing, and my shoulder was bleeding, and when our boots were removed we actually poured water out of them.

I had at least two more hours of drill to do for stealing strawberries from the school gardens. Strawberries were plentiful in Hampshire, and some of us would creep out of the barracks in the dead of night and go strawberry-picking. Unfortunately for me I left behind one of my socks with my name tag still firmly attached – hence the drill. I was not looking forward to doing another spell on the parade ground, but for some reason Billy never got round to dishing it out. If a cadet got four hours of drill he faced dismissal; I had three and a half hours, and nobody in the college wanted to be the person who sank my career.

A week later Sunshine and I were on guard duty at the main gate for one week with four other cadets. One day we were loaded into the college 10-ton truck and went to a naval barracks in Portsmouth to pick up fifty rifles. There was going to be a large parade at the college with the cadets forming a guard of honour.

The rifles were issued, and for the next few days the parade ground was full of marching and drilling cadets. I must say we all became very good at it.

The day of the parade arrived, bright and sunny. The college was full of visiting parents, relatives and naval and military personnel of every description. There was also a sprinkling of very pretty young women. The visitors took their seats and the parade started. Mercifully for me, I was not now in the 'colour party' from the guardroom, being too short, but Sunshine was. He had been given the task of raising the flag.

The colour party approached the flagpole with Sunshine as centrepiece, clutching the rolled-up flag fiercely to his chest. His boots almost had a shine on them.

The parade came to attention, and with a 'snap, snap' presented arms. Billy looked pleased. Sunshine and the colour party approached the flagpole, and Sunshine hitched the rolled-up flag to the halyard. The bugles blew, and the flag was hoisted smartly to the top. A roll on the drums, and the bugles sounded again. Sunshine pulled on the halyard to open the flag, which billowed out in fine style. Out of the flag fluttered a collection of condoms; there were also condoms stitched into the flag. Sunshine had been nobbled.

"Take it down, laddie, take it down," rasped Billy.

Titters ran round the gathered guests. The visiting admirals looked distressed – but not as distressed as the director, who looked like he might suddenly have a heart attack. The young ladies blushed, but I noticed one or two were trying not to laugh.

Somehow the situation was retrieved; the flag was re-hoisted and the parade was dismissed. It was never discovered who sabotaged the colour party. Sunshine swore that he picked the flag up from the rack, already rolled up and ready to fly. I had a good idea who had done the dirty deed, but Sunshine was certainly on parade that day.

Later that summer the time came for each cadet to choose the shipping line he would like to join. The majority went for the big companies of the day, Cunard, Royal Mail, Blue Funnel and Union Castle being among the favourites. Cadets tended to list an oil-tanker company as their third choice, to show bravado, but none really wanted to sail on a tanker.

I could not make my mind up, until one day a ship came up the Solent looking like a wounded beetle. Low in the water, she was black-hulled and dirty. She had a single tall funnel, which was known as a 'Willy Woodbine'. She crawled along, belching clouds of black smoke.

"What company is that?" I asked.

"Oh, that's the bloody Clan Line," a knowledgeable cadet cut in: "hell ships, bad feeders, always out in India and the Far East for months at a time. *Nobody* goes near those things."

I put the Clan Line down as my first choice. It was fate. I served with them for twenty-five years, reaching the rank of marine superintendent. The Clan Line bought out Union Castle and became the biggest shipping line in Britain, with over 130 ships, from passenger liners to tramps and tankers, and the small ships running across the North Atlantic to Canada with newsprint. This voyage was an experience never to be forgotten. It was 2,500 miles from the top of Scotland to Corner

Brook, but we always reckoned we did twice that going over every wave. All the big fashionable lines went to the wall long before the Clan Line finally stopped trading, and most of the lads who joined them ended up without a job.

The period from the mid sixties to the late seventies saw some of the most well-constructed and beautiful ships ever built grace the world's oceans. Most followed the traditional routes of the old sailing clippers. Eventually economics drove them from the seas, and by the early eighties they were all sold or scrapped, many ending up in China as coal hulks.

But I was privileged to sail on some of them. Oh, Lucky Jim!

WILLY WOODBINE

It was a wet and blustery day in Plymouth. I had finished at training college and now had to present myself at the Customs House on the Barbican for an eye test to get into the merchant navy. Several people failed this test, mainly because of colour blindness. This all should have been thought of before their parents had paid out loads of money for pre-sea college training.

I read through all the funny-coloured cards and the sight test, and then the examiner took me into a small room and turned the lights out. Standing behind a lantern I had to read the different coloured lights – white, red and green – as the clerk cranked a handle round. This was important as ships' navigation lights are red to port and green to starboard with white masthead lights. Normal colour vision is crucial when navigating a ship at night.

All I could see was a series of white flashes, but not wanting to disappoint I shouted out, "Red . . . green . . . red . . . er, white?"

The lights went up and, with a serious expression on his face, the clerk came round to the front of the lantern stand and informed me, "Things are not looking good for you, boy." He stood behind me. "Bloody hell – you are too short! You are looking under the light."

A couple of large books were produced and I stood on them. The lights went out, and bingo! all was revealed. I sailed through the test and my Board of Trade eyesight certificate was issued, dated January 1958.

So, I packed all my gear into two large trunks and set off for Newport, where I was to join the *Clan Macbeth*. As the ship was not berthing until the early hours I stayed in the Railway Hotel in Newport, where a revered sea captain told me to "Save, save, save, sonny, for your certificates and your pension." What a change in attitudes forty years has made!

Early next morning a taxi took me down to the docks. There were some large fine-looking vessels alongside, and the driver had to ask where the *Macbeth* was berthed. We rounded a cargo shed and there she was.

My face must have gone pale at the sight of her, and the taxi driver advised, "You will be all right there, boyo."

She lay alongside the quay streaked with rust and towering up out of the water, being empty of cargo. The most noticeable item was her funnel, tall and straight, black with two red bands round it – a Willy Woodbine. The gangway was almost vertical, and an overside discharge from the engine room was keeping it well wetted with spray. A circulating pump could be clearly heard from the quayside wheezing in the bowels of the engine room.

I struggled up with all my gear, to be met by the third mate.

"Welcome to the wreck of the *Hesperus*."

He was really trying to cheer me up.

"The seacunny will show you to your cabin."

The seacunny was a Bangladeshi. He was a helmsman or quartermaster on board.

The cabin was on the starboard side in the midships block and was quite large, with two bunks and a settee. A coarse coconut mat was all that offered for a carpet. There was no washbasin, but there was a shower and toilet for five officers and cadets at the end of the alleyway, right outside the engine-room door. A blast of oily heat came up out of the depths below – fine in the middle of winter, but it was to prove hellish in the tropics.

Going further forward I was introduced to the Captain and the chief steward and signed on to the ship's articles for two years. My wages were £8 a month, four of which I signed into an allotment note to be paid into my bank account.

"You will need that, laddie," said the steward, "for when you sit your ticket."

Young men on board could not have alcohol of any kind until they were twenty-one, but cigarettes and tobacco were extremely cheap. The fags came in tins of fifty, and I can still recall the marvellous smell from plug tobacco in a similar tin.

The third mate showed me around the ship, and the chief mate told me to get unpacked and report at 0600 hours the next morning for day work.

The *Macbeth* had been built in 1941 in Philadelphia and towed across the Atlantic to have her engine installed on the Tyne. She was single-screw, steam-reciprocating, with steam supplied by three water-tube Scotch boilers. On a good day she could just about make 10 knots. The decks were flush right along her length, with three cargo hatches forward. There was another small hatch between the bridge deck and the engine room (this had served as a coal bunker before the ship was converted to oil), and another behind the midship housing, making a total of five cargo hatches. Completely around the ship in the 'tween decks was the degaussing gear – a thick band of copper wires which when electrified was supposed to neutralise magnetic mines. I trusted it would never be needed.

The original idea was that the *Macbeth* would last about five years and see the war out, and yet here she was still trading in 1958.

The crew, all from Chittagong in Bangladesh, lived down aft, about six men per cabin. There were two galleys on the poop – one for the deck crew, and one for the engine staff. The cooks were called *bhandari*s, and worked on coal-burning stoves. Galleys were beautiful places to be in when the winter set in, but unbearably hot in the tropics.

For the officers, there were no fridges. Bread was kept in a large bin on deck, along with vegetables that would last about a week. There was a deep freeze. It had meat and fish mixed up in it, and was only opened once every few days. The Board of Trade allowance gave us four eggs a week, of which two would be used for cooking. The company stuck rigidly to this ruling.

A typical breakfast would consist of a cereal, which you flooded with water first to wash out the weevils. The water was drained off and powdered milk was then added. We each had one piece of toast, with a small pack of Kerrygold butter split between four of us.

Occasionally some fish was served, usually a fish curry and rice. If sausages were on the menu, they were split in half down the middle and one sausage was shared between two people. Bacon and eggs was on the menu maybe once a week.

Needless to say, after a few days the other cadet and I were starving; so we filled up at lunchtime with boiled potatoes and HP sauce.

The first night I was woken up in the middle of the night to sounds of merriment and laughter outside. I looked out of the forward porthole, and there on the hatch top a group of naked officers and young women were dancing round and round. It was snowing and freezing cold.

'Oh, boy,' I thought, 'this is the life for me!'

I went back to sleep again knowing I had to get up at six. The next thing I knew the third mate was shaking me awake.

"Are you OK?" he cried. "It's three in the afternoon."

He thought I was dead. Apparently the steam radiator was leaking and I had been slowly suffocating. Nobody had missed me until then. A fine start to shipboard life! Also the local dockers had gone on strike over the naked women running about the place.

"Embarrassment money, boyo!"

I reckoned they secretly wanted to join in.

I was put on duty observing the cargo going into the holds, and I had to report back to the officers anything going wrong. The engineer on duty asked me to let him know when the glands

27

on the pistons of the steam winches became so loose they needed to be tightened up again.

After a couple of hours of continually running back to tell him that such and such a winch was belching steam, I got hold of a spanner and went round and screwed all the piston glands up tight.

'That should fix it,' I thought. 'It needs a bit more organization around here.'

While I was sitting in the pantry having a cup of tea, the second engineer appeared. He did not look happy. Being Scottish, he was mouthing off at me in a funny language, but the gist of it was "What silly Sassenach bastard has screwed in all these piston glands?"

"Me," I stammered. "I thought it would help."

Two of the pistons were glowing blue-hot and had seized and others were on the way out. I never interfered with engineering matters again – not on that trip anyway.

So we sailed from Cardiff for Glasgow. A heavy swell was setting in from the Atlantic, and the *Macbeth* rolled her way up the Irish Sea, making me feel quite queasy.

Sailing up the Clyde past the shipyards and docks was most interesting. Sir James Watt's original steam engine was perched on the bank of the river, and the noise of riveting and the movement of cranes and machinery brought it home to me that this place was the centre of British shipbuilding and engineering skills. Little did I know that within a few years it would be virtually all gone.

Loading cargo commenced at a slow pace. Dribs and drabs of heavy machinery and cased goods appeared out of the dockside sheds and were loaded by a drab-looking bunch of men in heavy coats and flat caps. Then the whisky turned up. Immediately the dockers took on a more aggressive mood. We cadets were put into the cargo spaces to make sure none of the cargo was broached and stolen, but the word was that these men could steal a bottle of whisky from under your nose. They were up to every trick in the book. A wooden case of Scotch would be dropped on to its corner, breaking some of the bottles inside. With our attention taken by this event, the dockers were quickly stealing bottles elsewhere in the hold. It was not long before the whole deck was reeking of whisky – a smell that would be written into my mind for years to come. One of the men became so stupefied with drink that he was passed ashore on a flat tray by crane. There was a Norwegian watchman employed to stop such goings-on, but I am sure he was bribed to keep his head down, as nothing changed when we were loading whisky.

Every morning I would be dispatched to the company offices in Hope Street with the ship's box. This was a large black affair with the ship's name boldly stamped on it in white letters. It was kept padlocked, and all sorts of secret papers were inside – or so I thought. In fact, in my innocence all I was doing was transferring a few bottles of booze to the people in head office against customs regulations.

The trip up was by taxi, but I had to make my own way back on the bus and tram, and when I claimed a shilling in expenses the dour Scottish captain gave me threepence, "to make the laddie aware of the value of money".

At last we sailed by way of Port Said and all ports east to India.

The weather was bad in the Bay of Biscay, and at mealtimes everybody roped themselves in to the table. The *Macbeth* rolled in a slow, positive way, whilst the steady thump of the engine drove us along at about 8 knots. I was on watch, four on four off, and the need for sleep took over any thought of food. Coming off watch, I would be asleep before I hit my bunk.

If anything, the weather in the Mediterranean was worse than in the Atlantic – severe violent gales all the way to Port Said, with hail and freezing rain. Eventually we arrived, and the first sights and sounds of the East in those days were the slums and minarets of Egypt, de Lesseps' statue tipped over on its side, the continual cry of the bumboat men and the wailing of the muezzins in the mosques. The noise never stopped, even at night.

The bumboat men swarmed on board, and I was conned into parting with £1 for a large grapefruit by a filthy-looking Arab with one eye. It later turned out that the grapefruit had been filled with air from a bicycle pump and then plugged.

The Egyptians, who now ran the Suez Canal, had introduced a convoy system, much decried by the exiting British, but it eventually turned out to work incredibly well, in contrast with the British way of going down the canal from signal station to signal station and tying ships up on the canal bank to allow others to pass.

The signal stations, of which there were several, were spaced out down the length of the canal, and they were now used for relaying all forms of navigational information concerning the movement of shipping. I was fascinated by it all – a fascination which I always felt every time I passed along that famous waterway of which Joseph Conrad wrote, 'The French mind set the Egyptian muscle in motion and produced a dismal but profitable ditch.'

We sailed on into the Red Sea. To us 'first trippers' it was like stepping into a furnace. The heat was blistering, and there was no relief anywhere on board. Our legs turned red, and the pain was like a fire. We had no thought of skin cancers in those days. It was not long, though, before the skin hardened and I never suffered from burnt legs again. We lads, working on deck, became as brown as nuts and hard as iron. There was one problem, though – or really two. The first was dhobi itch – an itching rash in the armpits and groin caused by the heat and insufficient water to wash out clothing. The second was prickly heat. This also caused a rash, but the main problem was the stabbing pains in the back of the neck. To avoid heat exhaustion salt tablets were supplied. The engineers would down these by the handful as the temperature on the bottom plates often exceeded 120 degrees.

The cure for dhobi itch was Whitfield's ointment – a white greasy-looking goo supplied by the Board of Trade. My first attempt with this stuff I really was taken in.

"Rub it on round your nuts," I was advised by the engineers.

The next minute I was leaping about all over the decks. It was like someone had sprayed acid over me.

"You bastards!" I retorted, but it did clear up the rash.

I was more careful in future. It's funny, but you never hear of Mr Whitfield's ointment these days.

The ship called at Port Sudan, where the locals were known as fuzzy-wuzzies because of their long dreadlocks caked in camel dung. She also called at Assab, Djibouti and Berbera. All these places had just received or were about to receive independence from Italy, France, and Britain respectively. They were clean and orderly places and the locals appeared to be a happy lot. A few years later the Russians had influence in them and slaughtered thousands.

It took about a week in each port to discharge cargo; then we sailed across the gulf to Aden. Aden was still British, and there was a large base there. It was also a free port, and you could purchase all sorts of goodies at rock-bottom prices. But if I thought the Red Sea was hot, Aden beat it by a mile. The landscape was sand and rock and the sun's heat just bounced off it. Night seemed even hotter. The ship, being black-hulled, absorbed the heat during the day and threw it back off again after sunset. Sleep was just about impossible.

Several days later we cleared the harbour and set off across the Indian Ocean for Colombo. After a day or so it became much cooler, and we settled into a daily routine during the ten-day passage to Ceylon.

Arriving off Colombo, we were advised that we would be anchored for maybe two months waiting for a berth. The discharge rate in the port was incredibly slow, so we had to wait. We lads got one of the lifeboats down and did circular tours of the other ships in the anchorage. The captain of one of the Clan ships had built a motorized sampan, and every few days he would shoot off into the harbour, pick up the mail for all the ships from the agents and then come back out and deliver it. He was much appreciated, as mail is the most important thing in a sailor's life far from home.

After berthing many weeks later we started discharge, but only managed about 50 tons a day. A bunch of us formed a skiffle group and three times a week played on Colombo Radio. They offered us a contract, but we declined that one. Football was played in the blazing sun and humidity, and I remember one match where the water taps on the ground had been turned off, which made us delirious with thirst. I can still recall the little chap coming out at half-time with a huge jug of cold lime juice. It was delicious, but there was not nearly enough of it. The local team we were playing beat us twelve-nil, in bare feet.

At last we left Colombo and travelled up the east coast of India, discharging at exotic-sounding places like Allepey, Pondicherry, Koilthottam, Madras and Vizagapatnam. Then we sailed across the Bay of Bengal to Chittagong to finish discharge and then start loading before heading back to Britain.

Chittagong was hot, humid and full of flies, bugs and mosquitoes. Sleep was still virtually impossible. The crew were changed there, having been on board more than two years. Many of them only found out on arrival that they had lost relatives, or even whole families, since they had been gone. The new crew were picked by the agent and the three senior officers on board, and I soon realized that a considerable amount of bribery was going on in the selection of the crews. We lads were posted in the customs shed to search the outgoing crew's luggage for anything pilfered from the ship's stores. But how could you turn a man in for stealing, say, six bars of soap and a couple of pounds of sugar when he only earnt a few pounds a month and had maybe twelve kids to support?

The main cargo loaded in Bangladesh was jute for Dundee. It

came on board in huge bales, each weighing over 400 pounds. The men in the hold stowed it into place with six men to a bale, all armed with cargo hooks. As they sweated and swung the jute into position, they all sang a shanty in Urdu. Maybe after forty years these chants have disappeared along with the cargo hooks.

From Chittagong we sailed up the Ganges Delta to Chalna, for more jute, loaded this time from paddle-wheel barges in the river. Portholes had to be kept shut, as long bamboo poles would quickly lift anything worth having out of your cabin and on to the barge.

There was a Russian ship in the anchorage, and this ship played communist music and slogans over the Tannoy day and night, keeping everyone awake. Some of our lads got drinking with the Russian sailors, and during one visit to their ship one of our engineers cut the wire to the Tannoy system. The Russians could not find the break, so for the rest of our stay the Soviets were silent.

From Chalna we sailed for Galle in Ceylon to load tea. By this time the south-west monsoon was starting and the Bay of Bengal was rough; so we only managed about 5 knots. Arriving at Galle, we were taken in by a pilot; one anchor was dropped. We swung round, head to sea, and dropped the other anchor and then lay back and picked up six wires over the stern to mooring buoys. There we lay for three weeks.

Galle was a beautiful place. It had been colonized by the Portuguese and the Dutch. It was clean, with handsome buildings and glorious beaches. We all became members of the Galle Beach Club and would spend happy hours swimming in the sea. My membership was free as I was an apprentice. The cargo was sailed out to the ship in huge ocean-going dhows. These dhows were the regular transporters all over the Indian Ocean, especially to the Persian Gulf. The crews on them would lay the dhow smartly alongside, dropping the large lateen sail as they did so. The south-west monsoon was now pushing a heavy swell into the bay, and the dhows swooped and soared as they lay alongside, the men being most agile as they attached the chests of tea to the ship's cargo hooks and then swung them up and over the side by the derricks. It was fascinating work – something the world appears to have forgotten about. We loaded over 2,000 tons of tea in chests, as well as a considerable amount of other cargo.

In those days, loading ships in the Far East involved working out the space remaining in the holds. This was done by the ship's officers measuring up the areas in each hatch at the end of the day. The chief officer would then calculate from all the boat notes how much cargo was in the ship and the space remaining. A boat note was in fact a mate's receipt. It was a document produced by a small army of tally clerks (*babus*) who worked on board. They produced one note for every item of cargo. The notes had a financial value, the same as a mate's receipt and bill of lading. From the copies sent ashore a ship's manifest was made up, and on completion of loading this was handed to the master. Today all this is done in the twinkling of an eye by computer, but at that time it gave employment to many people.

Three weeks went by, and at last we sailed. The stern lines were cast off and the anchors shortened. Then, after heaving them home, we steamed slowly out into the ocean and turned the ship's head towards Aden and the Red Sea. Our passage would take us through the 10-degree passage near the Maldives. However, the south-west monsoon was now at its height, and as we proceeded further west the wind and gales became stronger, and the seas larger and heavier. Our speed went down from 8 knots to less than 5. The ship felt as though she was stopped in the water. She climbed every wave, burying her bow into the sea, the propeller rattling and roaring as the stern came out of the water. The engine had a governor on it, which would cut in when the screw started to race. Sometimes the governor stuck, and the engineer on watch could be heard belting it with a 10-pound mundy hammer, whilst the engine raced faster and faster, shaking the stern to bits. Progress was slow. Each noon our position on the chart was no more than 120 miles away from that of the previous day. For a couple of days we even appeared to be going backwards, only logging about 30 miles.

It was most galling to see some big, fast and powerful liner come up from astern and go ploughing past us at about 18 knots. Other Clan ships reported that they were 100 miles to the south of us and logging 7 knots. Would we ever get there?

Get there we did, and we took on fuel oil bunkers, stores, and more goodies from the duty-free bumboats. Aden Harbour in those days was crowded with shipping, nearly all British-flag vessels. A few years later it would all be gone, and the Russians would move in and slaughter thousands of the locals.

We sailed back through the canal and on to our first discharge port, Barcelona. My time at sea almost came to an abrupt end here.

The carpenter and the other apprentice and I went ashore. The Ramblas was heaving with bars, and girls. After six months in the Indian subcontinent, here we were enjoying the spoils, trolling from bar to bar. The time flew by.

One of the girls was determined to remind us she was 'international pussy'. That said it all.

"Christ," I said, "we had better get back – the ship is sailing!"

We grabbed a taxi and set off for the harbour, and, whether by mistake or design, the driver took us to the wrong berth. When we did finally find the right dock, the ship was lying about 20 feet off the quay with just head and stern lines out. The mate was just hoping we might make it back. A rope was thrown and we went over into the oily water and then up the pilot ladder and on board. The carpenter was put in the logbook and fined two days' pay, and we lads got a severe rocketing. The chief mate reckoned we would be in big trouble in Head Office in Leadenhall Street, but funnily enough I never heard any more about it.

The ship staggered its way back to London, averaging less than

5 knots all the way from India. The ship having been painted on the outside to make an impression to the owners in London, the last few days were spent painting the cabins out, especially the decks, with a Clan Line speciality, deck green. It had a peculiar smell, which lasted for days, and went very sticky in patches. Everything got covered eventually in green paint. The steam radiators went on as it got colder, which did not help the pong. When we opened wardrobes to take out blue uniforms, clouds of mosquitoes would fly out. So much for them only living twenty-four hours! The damp ruined clothing, and at that time it became the practice to fit a light bulb in the wardrobe to keep down the humidity, but after a few disastrous fires this practice was banned.

Arriving in King George Dock, London, I was informed I would be staying on board for three weeks' coastal work; then I would go home for ten days' leave. When you are eighteen years of age and enjoying yourself around the UK coast, who needs to go home?

There was literally a girl in every port. I met one in the Catholic Seamen's Mission in Hull. She was serving behind the bar, and was a vision of loveliness – blue eyes, blond curly hair and what looked like a lovely figure. We chatted over the Red Barrel and Courage beer pumps, and she appeared as keen as mustard. She kept coming back to me, flashing a smile, and holding me steadfast with her deep-blue eyes. I asked her out to the pictures, and she readily agreed.

It was with some excitement that I met her outside the Odeon cinema the next evening. She got out of the taxi and hobbled up the steps towards me. She had leg irons and a club foot. My desire diminished somewhat.

Sitting in the back row, the kissing started. My hand settled on her knee. She straightened her leg and, snap, the leg iron trapped my fingers like a vice.

I took her home in a taxi, and she invited me in. Her father worked on the trawlers, and when he heard I was off a ship in the dock he looked none too pleased. He and his wife went up to bed, and the Vision and I continued the kissing on the settee. Ten minutes went by and there was a loud knocking on the ceiling.

"Get that bloody sailor out of here!" from up above.

I left, nursing bruised fingers on my right hand.

Having no money left, I walked back to the ship through the freezing night, arriving back on board with the front of my camel-hair coat frozen as stiff as a board.

I saw the Vision many years later in one of the pubs in Hull. She was fat and puffy, and I only recognized her because of the club foot and leg iron.

When I arrived back in Sheepwash after nine months at sea, my mother enquired, "Did you enjoy the voyage, dear, and did you behave yourself?"

"Always, Mother, always."

I was ready for another voyage. I was hooked.

THE COUNTESS

It was in reality a pier-head jump. We had just come back from an eight-month voyage to India and all ports between. The ship was large, but slow, having a 2,000-horsepower engine in a 10,000-ton hull. She had been built in Philadelphia to carry cargoes across the Atlantic in the Second World War. There was no air conditioning; the cabins were small and airless. Months of heat, flies and mosquitoes with little sleep, and in port the continuous rattle of steam winches, night and day, made life exhausting. There was also the added discomfort of prickly heat, which produced a nasty rash and stabbing pains in the back of the neck. It was several years before the pains in my neck finally went away.

There were three of us lads. The senior had a cabin to himself, but we were all on 'four on, four off' at sea, and Chinese watches in port (six on, twelve off; twelve on, six off). There was very little in the way of fresh vegetables, and the freezer was only opened once a week for the meat and fish mixed up inside it. The three of us existed on potatoes and HP sauce, and curries from the *bhandari*s' galley down aft – fiery concoctions that blew your head off.

The senior trainee officer cadet was a shifty character called Paul, and he and the carpenter, or chippy, were mates. The chippy, because he was white, had officer status on board and lived in the cabin next to Paul. The two of them always had a plentiful supply of whisky, but we never asked where they got it.

I went home for ten days' leave and rejoined the ship in Liverpool, to be immediately told by the chief mate on board to report to the dock superintendent. So along I went to his office in the cargo shed. He was a kindly old gent – a very experienced seaman who first went to sea in sailing ships and gained a sailing master's licence.

He took one look at me and asked if I had been involved in stealing cargo on the ship – whisky and radios being the main items. I now realized what all those shifty-looking Indian gentlemen with bulging lungis were doing coming and going from the chippy's workshop.

"No, sir," I told him.

"Well, Head Office reckon you must have been. Paul and the chippy have been fired and Head Office want me to get rid of you as well. That will be your career at sea at an end. The carpenter will never work on a British ship again."

The sea was my life, and the thought of losing that life brought me up short.

"So, young man, you will get back on board, pack your gear and go across the dock to the *King George*. She sails tonight for South Africa, and worldwide tramping. By the time you get back here over a year will be gone and London will have forgotten all about you."

I thanked him profusely and scuttled back on board. It really was a pier-head jump.

That night we sailed. The owner's agent had scoured the Liverpool waterfront for a crew, and most of them, especially the deckies, were, to put it politely, the scum of the earth. There was another lad with me on board – a little Scotsman. We took an instant dislike to each other, which was not good as we shared a small cabin. I took the top bunk – it was always safer up there, out of harm's way.

The next afternoon we were out in the Irish Sea with a moderate gale blowing. It was cold and wet out on deck, but we had to hold the compulsory boat drill, and the second officer was calling the names out for the lifeboat I was in. He got no reply to "Ha'penny!"

"Ha'penny!" he called again. "Come on – one of you buggers is Ha'penny."

A surly individual with a spotty face stepped forward.

"The name is Halfpenny, Mr Mate."

It turned out his place of birth was marked down as Aintree Race Course.

I was put on a watch – four on, eight off. I couldn't believe it – so much sleep. On watch, I would steer for one hour, lookout for two, then spend another hour as 'farmer'. The farmer called the next watch and made the tea. There was no automatic helm, so we were in hand-steering all the time.

The *King George* had a full cargo for South Africa and Mozambique.

The first few days were the usual rough seas, and then at last we broke out into the warmer seas and weather off Gibraltar, and headed south for the Cape.

The crew were a bad lot, and several of the able seamen had it in their heads that we cadets were sneaking to the mates about them. One – a nasty bit of work called Snaky – came at me one afternoon behind the deckhouse and informed me he was going to 'punch the lights out of me'.

Two years of hard training and plenty of heavy manual work had made me very strong and fit, and as he rushed in I rattled him with two straight lefts and a right cross. He went down fast with a bloody nose. The other sailors gathered round, but an old Scouser called Billy calmed things down, and from then on we lads had no more trouble with the crew.

Discharge in Mozambique finished several weeks later, with the crew enjoying the delights of runs up the road in Lourenço Marques – a town with plenty of bars, nightclubs and restaurants and a fearsome secret police force if you got into trouble. The ship lost Snaky there, with a broken jaw in a fight in the Penguin Bar. I was promoted to AB and my wages went from £8 a month to £18, and an overtime rate of 3 shillings an hour thrown in. My Scottish pal was not too happy about this, and some time later we fought and were then put in separate cabins. I met him several years later on the beach in Durban. He had a wife and two kids and by then was a nice chap. We had a good laugh over that voyage on the *King George*.

She was a good sea boat in all weathers. She was flush-decked throughout, and could chug along at 13 knots. The deck housings were riveted to the main deck, and in heavy seas down off Cape Horn the rivets parted and the housing moved back 6 inches or more. The cabins all got wet from seawater getting in.

After discharging in Mozambique we went to Durban to load coal for a place called San Nicolas on the River Plate, Argentina.

It took about a week to load on the Bluff at Durban, the coal being tipped into the ship from railway trucks, 30 tons at a time. The noise and the dust were frightful, added to which was the smell from the whaling factory right astern of us. The dead whales were hauled up on a slip before being flensed by a villainous-looking lot of men with long knives on poles.

I was pleased when the ship was down to her full-load marks. Her position in the water showed off the best lines of her. We could load to 'tropical fresh'. Although it was wintertime where we were going, it was outside the 'winter zone' – just.

Sailing was a great feeling as we rounded the breakwaters off the Bluff, and then the fun started. With 8,000 tons of coal in her, the ship was very stiff. That is, she had too much bottom weight; so she rolled like a pig, even in a flat calm. By the time we were south of Cape Town in heavy seas she rolled continuously, 40 degrees one way, then 40 the other, all in less than ten seconds. Sleep was almost impossible, and the chairs in the saloon were all tied together to stop them flying away from the tables. The Scot and I had to go down into the holds twice a day to take the temperature of the coal, and, even though it was winter down south, every day the cargo got hotter and hotter. It became roastingly hot inside the hatches and we were getting temperatures over 100 degrees. The friction on the cargo due to the rolling was causing it to heat up. The Captain thought he would be clever and go down south near to Tristan da Cunha to save distance on a great circle, but after almost a week of horrendous weather the second mate persuaded him to put the helm up and go further north to seek better conditions.

One night I had just come off watch and turned in, roping myself into the bunk, when there was an almighty bang. The alarms bells rang, and everybody turned out. The heavy derrick on the foremast had broken its lashings and was swinging about in a crazy fashion, threatening to smash all around it. The second mate had immediately turned the ship with her stern to the seas, and the rolling was dramatically reduced.

"Right," bawled the mate, "I want volunteers to go out there and get that boom back and lashed."

The Scot was not keen, myself full of bravado from reading Joseph Conrad and C. S. Forester I went out with a Norwegian sailor and one of the Polish greasers. It was murder on the foredeck. Heavy seas were washing over the hatches, and the rolling made it difficult to keep from slipping over the side. Mercifully lifelines were rigged, and we lashed ourselves to these in the freezing weather and managed to throw a heavy rope gantline over the head of the boom, take it to one of the winches and heave it tight. The problem then was getting the boom back into its crutch.

"Why don't we lower it down on to the hatch?" I suggested.

The Irish second mate appeared. He agreed with that idea, and after getting more electrical power to the winches, the gears on the large boom were engaged. The brakes were released and slowly the huge derrick was lowered towards the hatch top. The rest of the deck crew, now that the danger of being seriously hurt had been reduced, appeared as if by magic with baulks of timber and the derrick was lowered on to them. An hour later all was secure, with plenty of lashings, rope and wire to keep the boom in place. The ship was slowly returned to her course, and the rolling started again, but the lashings held, and we squared away for the River Plate.

"Well done, sonny!" the second mate said, hauling me into his cabin for a well-earned drink – something I was not officially allowed until I was twenty-one. I felt a real sailor that night; I had achieved something that could take its place alongside the tales I had heard of sailors of long ago. Now for Argentina!

The mouth of the River Plate appeared out of the early morning gloom, about 25 miles wide, with fearsome sandbanks and bars. The flow of the river coming down against the tide made the channel buoys appear as though they were higher than we were. Two Argentinian pilots came on board (after a struggle) from a very small launch, and we headed upriver towards La Plata and Buenos Aires. But the first night, much to our surprise, we put into Montevideo in Uruguay, passing the wreck of the German battlecruiser *Graf Spee* on the way. Montevideo was a real sailors' town, with loads of bars and nightclubs, and we lost one of the stewards there (we sailed early the next morning and he failed to make it). No replacement was available.

We sailed up past Buenos Aires to San Nicolas. There was Pampas all around us, with gauchos herding cattle on horseback. The small villages we passed were very poor and rundown, and what few people we saw looked woefully poverty-stricken. San Nicolas was a power station. All the way upriver, about 200 miles, when not on watch we were stripping the hatches ready to discharge the coal. Sure enough, when we opened No. 3 Hatch the heat almost blew the lids off, and as the shoreside grabs took the first of the cargo out it burst into flames. This apparently was normal on ships carrying coal in those days.

The crew now set about the serious business of enjoying themselves after the long voyage. The young deck boy, or peggy, was sent up the road with money and came back with several cases of spirits and beer. The Captain, Typhoon Lewis, and the mate, whom we called Pussyfoot, were not used to the ways of a white crew and they allowed the drink to come on board. The second mate was incensed.

"There will be trouble now, boyo," he growled, "just you wait and see."

Sure enough, the next morning the deckies and the stewards were insensible with drink. Some of them had been drinking Anise Liqueur (a drink that addles the brain) by the pint. We now had to put the fire hoses into the mess room to try to clean the place up and restore order. It was impossible – they were too far gone. And go they did, for that afternoon they all went ashore and the following morning the agent came on board to inform the Captain they were all in the calaboose. This now made our work even harder. The hatches had to be washed down and cleaned out and all the hatch beams and slabs had to be put back before we could sail. We worked for thirty-six hours straight to get the work done.

Just before we sailed I went on the dockside to read the draught marks and met two divers who had just come out of the exit water pipes from the power station. This was incredibly dangerous work in the fast-flowing river; the visibility in the water was nil. They were both Italian but could speak good English. One told me that in the war they had driven a manned torpedo into Alexandria Harbour and placed it right under HMS *Queen Elizabeth*, a battleship. The Royal Navy caught them, but they refused to say where the torpedo was. The navy then put them right down in the bowels of the ship in the hope they would come up with the position of the explosive. They kept quiet, and a huge explosion blew the bottom out of the ship. She settled on the mud, where she stayed for almost two years. Who said the Ities were cowards?

Before we sailed for Rosario, further downriver, I was detailed off to go ashore to the jail and take the seven crewmen in it by bus to Rosario. The jail was just a concrete wall, to which they were chained. Most looked terrible, with bruised and battered faces. They were taken to the bus, a dilapidated banger, and handcuffed to the seats. I sat in front with the driver and two policemen. I am sure that bus had only three wheels, and one of those was the steering wheel. We rattled and banged our way down dirt roads towards Rosario, 100 miles away.

After several hours my drunken compatriots needed to get out for food and whatever, and as it was approaching siesta time, the cops needed some lunch as well. We drew up in front of a seedy-looking cantina, and the men were released and led inside. The beers started going down in true British style, and it was not long before they and the police were thoroughly drunk. I went out to get the driver fired up, and when I returned to the bar all of them had gone and the two cops were handcuffed to the toilet. They now wanted to throw me in the pokey, but after a lot of argument they let me and the driver go on to Rosario. The driver stopped after a few miles and took off across the Pampas taking the keys of the bus with him. I was now well and truly up the creek.

Suddenly along came a vehicle driven by a gaucho with a horse in the back of it. He agreed to drop me off near to town.

I climbed in with the horse, which promptly tried to bite me in the back of the neck all the way to Rosario.

Arriving at the dockside at one o'clock in the morning, but there was no ship. I spent the night asleep in a grain elevator.

I was woken up early in the morning by the most frightful noise, and, looking out from my lofty perch, I could see that the road was full of troops and tanks. People were being frogmarched away, and several dead bodies lay in the pavé. Holy cow, another revolution! I did not know whether it was the Peronists or the other lot. Don't cry for me, Argentina! The disturbance went on all morning, until suddenly out in the river a huge battleship appeared. It looked like an old British one. Its guns were lowered and pointing towards where I was. This was getting serious.

There was an awful lot of shouting and jabbering going on amongst the army people on the dock; at about three o'clock in the afternoon, much to my relief, they all disappeared – even the battleship. I spent another night in the elevator, creeping out to get some water from a tap on the shed wall.

After another cold night I was relieved to see the *King George* dock early the next morning. The Captain and mate were beside themselves because I had lost most of the crew. Never mind getting involved in a local punch-up!

For the next three days the Scot and I and the only three deckies left worked with the chippy in the hatches from six in the morning until ten at night, rigging shifting boards and making feeders before we loaded a full cargo of grain for Nagoya in Japan.

The fourth engineer and I quickly found a couple of girls ashore, and after work we would go to the nightclubs with them for dancing – or that's what they called it. Unfortunately my girl's mother came along as well, as chaperon. On the dance floor it was pitch-dark, so she couldn't see what was going on, but I am sure she knew. To this day I often wonder what about thirty people were doing on that dance floor standing up!

We loaded a full cargo of bulk grain in Rosario and then set off for Buenos Aires to load a few thousand tons of bagged grain to top the loose grain off. There was still no sign of our missing men, so even the mates now had to stand in as helmsmen, and help with opening and closing hatches.

Buenos Aires – what a town! Bars and nightclubs by the hundred! The Copper Kettle, a lively bar, was well known amongst sailors worldwide in those days. There was a girl in there called Sapphire who had filed her teeth to points, top and bottom. Her party piece, if anybody turned her down, was to bite through an ear lobe or bottom lip.

One night, we moved from bar to bar. Having hardly any money, I became expert at cadging drinks. We ended up in a place near the Grand Theater and the Pink Palace. This joint was really upmarket, and we knew we would not last long in it. Well-heeled Argentine men and very beautiful women cruised the dance floor. The fourth engineer and I sat in a corner nursing a couple of beers.

The waiter came over and said, "One more and you're out."

At a table nearby was a very elegant woman. She turned to look at me, and I was shocked to discover she looked about ninety years old. Her face was lined and scarred, the skin like parchment. Her clothes had seen better days, and she wore a small pillbox hat with some gaudy feathers in it. She spoke impeccable English, and asked if we boys would like a beer. I went across to her table and she offered her hand, and as I bent to kiss it (as was the custom in Latin American countries) I noticed how calloused it was, and the fingers were all broken and twisted.

The waiter appeared with some beers.

"I want paying tonight, Countess, before you go."

He was most rude to her, but she elegantly laughed it off.

"As always, dear boy, as always."

She then started to tell me her story. She was indeed a countess, a Polish one. Her family had huge estates in Poland before the war, but when the Nazis came they took everything, including her father and brothers, whom she never saw again. She learnt later that the Russians shot them in the Katyn Forest along with 40,000 other Polish officers. She and her mother and two sisters were taken and sent to a concentration camp. She never saw her mother and sisters again. Torture and beatings were an everyday occurrence, but because of her good looks she was put in the camp brothel. Her story went on and on, and got worse. She was eventually befriended by an SS officer just before the war ended, and he had her sent to Ravensbruck concentration camp, which the Allies were fast approaching. She survived, just, and eventually made her way to Spain. She worked in the brothels in Barcelona, and managed to get a ship to Argentina, where she had been ever since.

The fourth engineer thought she was spinning us a line, but she turned an arm up and there was her camp number tattooed on her wrist.

"I have seen Martin Bormann and Eichmann here in BA," she whispered. "I told the authorities, but they threatened to put me in jail. They are all Nazis here in Argentina. I still work as a prostitute – it is the only thing I know. I cannot cry – it is impossible for me to do so."

I looked at her and said, "I cannot help you. I have no money and I am British and not here for very long."

The Countess handed me a piece of paper. On it was the name and address of a man in New York and a message written in Spanish and Polish.

"Tell this man. He always said he could help me."

I took the note and later passed it on to the Polish Embassy in London. The man did help her and she appeared in a film about Josef Mengele, the Angel of Death in the Nazi camps. She died in 1965, aged thirty-eight.

We went back to the ship, quite sober, and sailed for Japan the next morning.

IBN Khallikan, *south-west monsoon, Indian Ocean, July 1978.*

Columbia Star, *at the Captain's table.*

On the bridge of Hijaz, 1984.

Tauranga, January 1990.

Afric Star.

Sydney 1998 retirement presentation from Blue Star, 1998.

Clan Brodie. *(By courtesy of www.fotoflite.com)*

Scottish Ptarmigan. *(By of courtesy www.fotoflite.com)*

Clan Macbeth. *(By courtesy of www.fotoflite.com)*

THE MEKON

We sailed south from the River Plate with 8,000 tons of loose and bagged grain on board. The feeders in the 'tween deck, huge wooden boxes built through into the lower holds, had 100 tons of grain in each. As the cargo settled in the lower holds, the grain in the feeders would move down to keep the stow topped up to avoid shifting in heavy weather.

The plan was to take the shortest route to Japan: down to Tierra del Fuego, through the Magellan Strait, up the Chilean coast to Valparaíso for bunkers, then across the Pacific to Nagoya.

Unfortunately it did not work out like that. When we arrived off the Magellan Strait it was foggy and wet and we were advised there would be no pilots for two days. The strait in fair weather offered panoramic scenery, but the channel was full of hidden dangers and many parts were uncharted. The saving though, in time going round the bottom of Chile and Argentina was two days. The second mate advised the Captain to cut his losses and run back to the Cape of Good Hope, then head across the Indian Ocean and so to Japan. This would add almost a week to the voyage.

Typhoon Taffy would have none of it. Round the Horn we would go through the roughest seas in the world. Down there the winds blow for 12,000 miles around the world with nothing in the way to stop them. Depression after depression is the norm, with about four to five days between each. We were all gripped with that fear of the unknown which affects all sailors who ever sail in those waters.

We started to make preparations for heavy weather. All the ventilators on deck were unshipped and plugged; a canvas cover was securely lashed around the top of each vent. Extra lashings were then put on the anchors, the derricks and the lifeboats. All loose gear in the engine room and storerooms was lashed down and we prepared for Cabo de Hornos, the most southerly point of land in South America. The ship would be only 100 miles north of the loose icebergs called growlers, any one of which can sink a vessel.

We rounded the Horn early one morning, its forbidding cliffs rising up out of the sea as much as to say, "Welcome. Come and crash on to me."

There was a sigh of relief from all on board as we sailed into the seas beyond and headed north – maybe we had got away with it.

We were in for a rude shock. Within a day, although now steaming to the north-west, the ship was in a mountainous swell, with at least a mile between the tops of each wave. There was no wind but the barometer was going straight down.

The Norwegian sailor said, "Now ve get vind, strong body."

On watch early the next morning, it was black dark, with just the hiss of the huge waves passing under the ship. Suddenly from out of the night came a most fearful cry.

"Christ, what was that?" I said from my position on the bridge wing.

"Most likely an albatross or even a whale," the second mate replied.

Sailors of long ago had heard it, and it put the fear of God into them. It sure put the wind up me. At six in the morning the wind came, hissing across the surface of the ocean. There were slivers of white at first in small wavelets, but then within the hour the seas were growing into huge waves and breaking at their tops.

The ship was now moving heavily, pitching up and down fifty

feet or more and heavy seas were being thrown right across the decks and hatches. The lifelines had been rigged, but the order went out: 'No one out on deck.'

Rolling became worse, and course had to be altered all the time to ease the working of the ship, which was barely making 2 knots through the water. I was on the wheel in the afternoon, when a mountainous sea appeared on our port side, blotting out the leaden sky. It hit the ship with a tremendous crash. When the water cleared, both port-side lifeboats had gone, smashed to matchwood. The deckhouse was sprung away from its rivets, and water was pouring into the cabins on the main deck. We eventually had to repair the housing with the sailor's friend, a cement box, round the outside, until dry-docking could enable us to complete the job. But worse – the ship had taken a heavy list to starboard. The Norwegian and I were sent off to inspect the holds, and down in No. 3 Hatch we found the bagged cargo, about 1,000 tons of it, had shifted towards the starboard side, smashing the two feeders in the square of the 'tween deck to smithereens.

The wind was now blowing about 100 knots, with a howling sound like nothing on earth. It was as though the roof of the sky was being torn off.

"Now she is proper strong body," the Norwegian ventured. "Big trouble coming."

The lack of deck sailors in the crew now became apparent. We needed muscle, and plenty of it. As many volunteers as we could manage, which included a steward and two of the greasers, went down into the hatch, and we started moving the hundredweight bags of grain back across to the port side. The Scot was kept on the bridge, to take his turn on the wheel and to act as a lookout. There were only four sailors left from the original deck crew, so about eight of us worked to re-stow the cargo whilst outside the storm was reaching its full fury.

The work went on all night and until lunchtime the next day, and in that time we must have shifted at least 500 tons. Exhausted we went back up on deck. The sight that greeted us was awe-inspiring.

The seas towered up higher than the funnel, and were roaring away to leeward like express trains. The howl of the wind drowned out all conversation, and inside the deckhouse I found a frightened group of officers and the Captain's wife huddled in the saloon. Some were praying.

I met the second mate coming down from the bridge.

"I have persuaded Taffy to turn back for the Horn. Warn the bosun and everybody to secure everything, including themselves. We will turn the ship. Then you come up on the bridge."

I did his bidding and made my way gingerly up the ladders to the wheelhouse, at one stage hanging on and looking straight down into the water.

"Right, you take the wheel."

John, the second mate, seemed to be in charge of everything.

The Captain and the mate watched the ocean, waiting for a moment when they felt there was a chance. At last there was a slight lull in the huge waves crossing our bows.

"Hard a-starboard," he said to me on the wheel.

She came round so slowly it was agonizing, swooping and diving down across the waves. This was the most dangerous moment. She could have rolled right over. A huge wave smashed into the port side, but it had the effect of pushing her round a bit more quickly, although solid seawater came swilling through the wheelhouse door, shorting out the gyrocompass. Now we were steering a magnetic course.

Then she was round and heading south-east towards the Horn. The ship was water planing, the waves were so big and some were coming over the stern and flooding the afterdecks. The steering flat was well battened down, and hourly inspections were made from the engine room to check we were not taking water in there. If the steering engine failed, that would be it. We were now 'running the easting down', and the main problem was keeping her on a straight course to avoid broaching to and rolling over. It was extremely tiring for the man on the wheel to maintain our course, but the weather slowly improved from storm to severe gale. Normal watches were resumed and I managed to get some supper and a bit of a lie-down in my bunk.

By midnight there was an even greater improvement in the weather. The barometer was on the way up again and the wind had settled down to a gusty roar. The Horn was 200 miles away, and we passed it the next afternoon.

"Not many people get to see the Horn twice in a week, sonny boy. I bet you will never do that again," the second mate predicted. "Now we won't get past Durban without bunkering."

Durban was eighteen days away. The passage back across the Southern Ocean was rough – very rough – it being wintertime, but the sea was behind us and we made good progress. The ship was on a great-circle course and we passed close to Tristan da Cunha, a British colony. It looked a lonely, forbidding place and was soon to be abandoned for a while owing to an earthquake. Albatrosses followed us for thousands of miles, rarely landing on the ocean. They would glide up the side of the ship in the air currents, a beady eye watching us from a few feet away. Their wing span was more than 8 feet, and they never appeared to move their wings at all except when landing or taking off. Each bird had a tiny drip of water on the end of its beak – an indication that all was well with them.

After two weeks, land was sighted near the Cape and we made our way towards Durban, where we would take bunkers, water and stores. The bunker berth was on the Bluff, across the dock from the main part of town. The Captain gave shore leave until six in the evening.

Big mistake! By midnight none of the crew had come back. Durban could be a bad place in certain parts, especially down in Point Road, The Smugglers Inn being a notorious bar. Another saloon, The Criterion, had one bar in the dock and another in Point Road, and it was one of the only public houses in the world with a customs officer sitting between the two bars. He was usually a one-striper, and he was kept well oiled with free Cape smoke brandy. We knew our lot would be somewhere in this area. The second mate and I were sent ashore to try to get them back, and we travelled across to the main docks in a small ferry. It was a dark night and it was raining.

Some of the crew were found, insensible in The Smugglers Inn; the others we were told were in Addington Hospital. The dock police said they would get the drunks back on board whilst we went up to Addington for the others. We found three of them being treated in the casualty department, and the nurse said she might have some more on a ward, if we could identify them. Two men had been beaten unconscious and their faces were unrecognizable, but I knew one was ours by his luminous pink socks. I had no idea about the other one.

We were still short of two able seamen, the second cook and a steward, and there was no one available ashore to replace them.

We sailed the next day, after a two-day stay in Durban, for Singapore. The owners and charterers were not happy with Taffy one little bit.

We sailed across the Indian Ocean and through the Lombok Strait to Singapore for more bunkers. The weather was better now, with hot sun and plenty of rainstorms to wash the ship down and remove the salt of the southern seas.

I was quite surprised when we sailed without losing any more of the crew in Bugie Street, a notorious place full of low dives and bars. We cleared the Horsburgh Light at the entrance to the Malacca Strait and headed up the China Sea towards the east coast of Taiwan.

I was on deck, working with the crew, when a whirring noise was heard directly overhead. Looking up, we saw small, dark shapes tumbling across the sky, and over on the horizon flashes from warships firing their guns. We were in a Royal Navy firing range, and our crazy radio officer had failed to receive the warning. The Royal Navy sent a frigate charging across to clear us out of it. There was no such thing as VHF radio in those days. I found it all extremely exciting to be under shell fire.

Now our troubles all started again. It was the typhoon season in the Western Pacific, with on average over twenty-five storms in any one year. Typhoon Taffy now lived up to his name. He managed to get us close to at least two storms, and at one time we had warnings of five. Everything on board was battened down again, and we lived in a state of nervous tension until we reached Nagoya.

Japan in 1960 was still coming out of the ravages of the Second World War. Many of her people were still primitive and lived from day to day. The dock and factory workers still wore khaki uniforms with military-style helmets, and they all did marching exercises on the quayside before they started work. They seemed very militaristic and we often thought they could turn back into a great power.

A run ashore in those days was fantastic for us Europeans. One English pound would give you over 1,000 yen. You would be lucky to get 200 today. There were plenty of bars, mainly influenced by the large American Army presence in Japan. We officers found a small bar, and the owners, Mama San and Papa San, made it our home for the week we spent there. The Japanese loved the British, which was strange considering how badly they treated our boys in the war. They all tried to be like an 'English gentleman'.

Just before we left Nagoya, Mama San and Papa San gave us a party and sent each and every one of us on our way with a present. I still have the beautiful handmade Japanese doll they gave me. When I returned to Nagoya in 1978, the place where that bar had been had been turned into a container terminal.

Japanese Immigration gave us an extra deckhand as we sailed. He was an odd character, and what was known in those days as a 'remittance man'. In other words he bummed his away around the world with money sent to him by his family. This character had been trying to sell encyclopedias in Japan and had run foul of the law. They got rid of him as soon as a British ship turned up and would take him. This chap regaled us with stories as we sailed 'light ship' – that is, with no cargo – across the Pacific to Vancouver for a cargo of timber. The man had done everything from sheep farming in New Zealand to fighting as a mercenary in the Congo.

He was on watch one night when the mate reported him missing. The weather in the North Pacific at that time of year was always foggy for a couple of thousand miles or more. The ship was searched, but no sign of him could be found; so we turned round and at low speed retraced our steps. Twelve hours and we found nothing, so course was resumed for Vancouver, but suddenly someone spotted him swimming along in the ocean. He was hauled on board after being in the sea for nearly eighteen hours, but he appeared none the worse for wear, although the sea was pretty cold. When asked how he fell over the side, he replied that he didn't, but he felt like a swim – an unlikely tale. The second and I reckoned maybe he was pushed.

There was more to this man than met the eye; when we came alongside in Vancouver a posse of Mounties were waiting on the quay. They came on board straight away with the port authorities and our keen swimmer was taken away in handcuffs. He had been long wanted in Canada for serious crimes committed some time before. Now we were short-handed again.

The next six weeks we sailed between numerous ports in British Columbia, loading sawn planks – Nanaimo, Shermanus, New Westminster and a host of other small places in the Puget and Queen Charlotte Sounds. It was autumn – or fall, as they call it in Canada – and the scenery was stunning amongst the mountain passes with the trees turning to brilliant reds and golds. As we went through some of the narrow passes, Indian teepees could be seen, with large Cadillacs parked outside. In many of the bars and pubs we went in it was tragic to see the drunken state some of these Indian people got themselves into. The white man had introduced them to alcohol when settling in Canada, and many of them were still hooked on a booze culture.

Then we were fully loaded, and ready to sail. The timber was piled high across our decks with special chain lashings so that it could be released over the side in an emergency. The crew, now egged on by the Canadian dock workers' union, refused to sail until walkways were built on both sides of the deck cargo, instead of just on the starboard side. This dispute dragged on for three days, and eventually at great expense the additional wooden walkway was fitted. Meanwhile another problem cropped up: our crazy radio officer lapsed into a coma and was then pronounced unfit to sail owing to a chronic stomach illness. The ship could not sail without a 'sparky', so we went out to anchor to await a replacement. The man (I think it was a man) duly arrived. He was dressed in a green tracksuit with pink sneakers. He was (or said he was) American. On his head he wore a huge Stetson with coloured ribbons rove in it. His knowledge of radio was limited, but he had a piece of paper to say he was qualified, so we sailed for the Panama Canal and Avonmouth. The 'sparky' was indeed odd, to say the least. When he removed his hat we saw that he had a huge bald head with a protruding forehead. We promptly nicknamed him 'the Mekon' after a character in the *Eagle* comic, in the Dan Dare stories.

As we approached Balboa and the Panama Canal the weather became extremely hot and the Mekon started to complain about the lack of air conditioning on the ship. He appeared on the bridge one morning with a towel full of ice wrapped around his head. He was groaning about the heat being too much.

He was not very good on the Morse key, and we were sure he was missing a lot of messages. Sure enough, in Balboa a surveyor came on board with a list of complaints for the Captain. There was some doubt whether it was wise to leave the canal with the Mekon on board, but we did and it was to prove embarrassing later in the voyage.

Passing through the canal was never without incident. The machines that pulled a ship through each locks were called mules, and by careful mismanagement we managed to pull one of these off its track and into the canal. The driver narrowly escaped drowning, being swept astern and almost under the propeller. An investigation was held when we arrived at Colon, but it was proved that one of the two pilots and the driver got their orders mixed up.

It was now November as we sailed into the Caribbean. The hurricane season was over, but we had the gales of the North Atlantic to look forward to.

The next day (Sunday) was my twenty-first birthday. I asked the Captain for a case of beer to celebrate, but the Welsh bastard would not give me one as he said I was not twenty-one until the following day, and he was not going to break the rules: no drink until you are twenty-one, and even then no spirits.

The Mekon now started to play up. He would appear outside the radio room in bright-pink shorts and a yellow shirt, and on his head was a baseball cap with a radio aerial attached, on the end of which a ping-pong ball dangled, bouncing in the breeze. The man had a crazed smile on his face.

"I am a supreme being," he would claim, "and I want respect."

This performance went on for several days; then the mate found him grovelling on the deck and foaming at the mouth. He had delirium tremens. To you and me, drunk.

He was lashed into his bunk, for his and our safety, and the second mate and I managed to grapple with the radio communications. At that time I could receive and send Morse at about twelve words a minute, and the second mate was good at sorting out the stations and wavelengths. A fully trained 'sparky' would be receiving messages at twenty-eight words a minute, so we were soon identified as being in trouble. The radio watch in Portishead in England realized this and did their best to help out.

Once we passed into the high latitudes in the Atlantic the weather turned against us. There were heavy seas and a big swell. The ship did not roll, but went up and down as though in a lift. Having a timber cargo, she was just like a floating block of wood.

The deck cargo got wetter and wetter. Eventually, as we lost stability, we took on an angle of loll of about 15 degrees, and it was decided by Taffy and the mate to flood a lower hold with seawater to get some stability back into the vessel. This was done and the situation improved, but the timber in that hatch was now caked in salt.

At last we reached Avonmouth. We were towed in with a 10-degree list, but we had not had to jettison any deck cargo. Discharge started straight away and I was advised I would not be going home on leave, but would sail around the coast with the ship. I had only been away eleven months – who needs a spot of home leave!

There was a reason for this, though. Taffy took the sailors to court at his own expense over the cost of building the walkway in Nanaimo, and I was called as a witness. After all the grief that crew had caused during the voyage, I was only too pleased to help. The Captain won his case and the crew members involved had money deducted from their wages to cover costs. They all swore to get me one day.

The Mekon was carried ashore on a stretcher, still claiming his rights. The second mate went on to become a senior master in the company, and I went home to sit my examinations for second mate. Because I had been sailing as an able seaman the owners refused to pay me my £40 bonus on completion of my apprenticeship. I was still desperately short of money, but the Merchant Navy Officers Association (or trade union to some) took up my case, and within days I received my cheque.

I took my exams in the Dock Road examination centre, off the Commercial Road, in the East End of London – a forbidding place. To pass you had to obtain 700 marks out of a possible 1,000; so standards were very high. The written papers took three days to complete, and they were followed by oral and signalling tests. A failure in any of the three meant you had to try all of them again inside two weeks; further failure in any meant a return to sea for at least three months before trying again.

The examiner said to me during my orals, "Ever been round the Horn, sonny?"

"Yes," I replied proudly, "twice."

SCRAP VOYAGE

The *Clan Brodie* was what sailors call 'a steam up and downer'. She had twin screws with two reciprocating engines, and was originally powered from five water-tube Scotch boilers. Unfortunately, owing to the hammering she received from being a submarine depot ship in the Second World War, she was now reduced to three boilers and could only manage a plucky 12 knots. In wartime she could easily make 19 knots.

I joined her as a newly qualified third mate, with a fresh second mate's certificate.

She was well constructed and, for the Captain and deck officers, the cabins were well fitted out and comfortable. There was a large dining saloon and lounge. For the engineer officers it was a different story. Their cabins were on the port side, directly over the engine room in a long alleyway open at both ends. The deck moved away with a large camber, which meant they needed ladders to get up into the narrow coffin bunks. In bad weather the seas would thunder down the alleyway, flooding the cabins with water to a couple of feet or so. It was advisable to remove clothing from the bottom drawers before the bad weather set in.

Glasgow was freezing cold – ice and snow was the order of the day – but after a few days the weather cleared and we eventually started loading cargo for East Africa. Then, with about 2,000 tons in the ship, word came that there was 6,000 tons of bagged sugar in Gdynia, Poland, and we (the nearest available ship) were to go and load it. The owners were always keen to accept the offer of a lucrative cargo. Why the freight was so high became apparent as the voyage progressed.

Round the top of Scotland we went, battling north-westerly gales, which nearly put us ashore several times. The engines thumping away down below managed to keep us out of trouble, and we eventually cleared the Pentland Firth and headed out across the North Sea. The weather was vile. Massive seas and driving snow made life on the bridge almost impossible. At this time being down in the heat of the engine room was a bonus, but we deckies suffered from the extreme weather in the almost open wheelhouse. Navigation was by dead reckoning and the occasional sun sight.

We had some real characters on board amongst the officers. Charlie, the Captain, was known as the 'Welsh Git', for obvious reasons. The mate was 'Quarter Can Kid' because if he did ever give you a beer, he split the can four ways. The second mate was 'Vasco', after the famous navigator. His claim to fame was upsetting a box with £2,000 of silver coin in it all over his cabin deck. We were still finding them weeks later. My nickname I have conveniently forgotten.

Amongst the engineers, the chief was a reclusive Welshman. He kept sending into the company old but good boiler-water samples, so they never knew how bad the boilers really were. Then there was 'One Ball Willy' and 'Porteus' and 'Jesus', because he looked like him. Another was known as the 'Black Turd' as he was always covered in oil, which he never seemed to wash off.

The radio officer, or sparky, was Scottish and went by the name of Mcanurney, but he was known to one and all as the 'Nurnee'. He was a heavy drinker, though never so drunk that he couldn't operate his equipment. He had a considerable number of girlfriends in ports all round the United Kingdom, South Africa and Australia. He had been engaged to be married to a lovely girl in Durban, but when I met him this was all falling apart as he had made her sister pregnant. The Nurnee treated this as just another incident between alcoholic hazes. I met the girl's father later in Durban, and this man had murder in mind.

The chief steward was a sly, evil-looking character. He lived and worked in the officers' lounge, and sat there with his belly flowing over the table, playing patience continuously. The grease marks from his wrists were still there when we finally left the ship. He fed us – just – but the food was a little better than on other ships I had sailed on.

The crew were all from Bangladesh, and our quick exit from Glasgow prevented several of them from jumping ship and losing themselves in places like Bradford and other towns with large Asian populations.

When we entered the Skagerrak our problems really started. It was wintertime and the Baltic was freezing over. We managed to push our way past Kiel through moderate ice, but then we came to a grinding halt in good thick stuff. It was useless trying to get through it; we would have punched a hole in the hull. The Welsh Git called for a tug ice-breaker, and after a lot of argument a strange-looking vessel hove into sight and demanded cash to tow us into Gdynia. There was much shouting to and fro between the Welsh Git and the Polish captain on the tug. Poland was still a deeply communist state in the early 1960s, and the Polish trusted nobody, so it was several days before we finally berthed in Gdynia.

Gdynia was a drab, dreary town. The buildings still showed the scars of the last war. Virtually every one of them had shell and bullet holes covering the facades. The people looked poor and downtrodden, shuffling along the streets as though in a daze. There were several drunks staggering about the pavements and waving imaginary machine guns at us in particular.

Two armed soldiers were placed at the foot of the gangway and we were forced to sign ourselves on and off the ship. These soldiers were well wrapped up against the cold, and after a few days they relented from their stern outlook and came on board one at a time for a plate of curry and hot tea. All sterling on board was supposed to be surrendered to the ship's bond, and we were meant to buy Polish zlotys at sixty-five to the pound, but on a tip-off we bought £5 worth and hid the rest of our sterling on board.

The first night in, a 'raiding party' went up the road to test the market. They came back in the early hours in high spirits. There were plenty of bars and nightclubs all doing a roaring trade. The Americans had their own berth in Gdynia, and there were never less than three ships on it, and the crews were ashore with plenty of money in their pockets.

The raiding party reported that 200 zlotys could be exchanged for a pound note in any of the bars, so the next night a more determined and experienced gang of partygoers hit the high street. In the Polana bar, a visit to the toilet with some shady-looking individuals produced an exchange of over 300 zlotys for a pound note. The lads were in clover – beers and meals for next to nothing.

The dance floor was crowded and the Polish girls were all trying to get themselves a promise of marriage to American sailors. This all seemed rather odd. The Yanks were dead set against any trade with communist regimes, and yet the United States lines had their own berth in Gdynia.

The night progressed. Nightclub acts of a very high quality helped the party along and everybody was having a great time. Suddenly it all went quiet and into the room strode two men in heavy black leather coats, jackboots and homburg hats – the local Gestapo, or secret police. They were there to check up on the clientele. Striding around the dance floor, they stared severely at one and all, especially us foreigners.

Porteus and Willy got up, weaved across the floor, bowed low in front of the two thuggish-looking men and asked them to dance. The place erupted in laughter. Mercifully the Gestapo-types took it well. I had visions of thumbscrews at dawn.

The Poles had a good system. If you got drunk and caused trouble they locked you up for the night in a bare cell with no heat or food of any kind. If you did it again, jail for six months was the norm.

Cargo-loading started. Bags of sugar were swung into the ship by the most ugly and bad-tempered crane drivers. They turned out to be female, and a hard-looking bunch they were too. Then orders came on board that the owners now had arranged for a cargo of special heavy lift machinery and we had to leave a hole in the square of the hatches. This was to be loaded in Middlesbrough, so the bags had to be 'shored off', or 'tommed', with timber for the passage back across the North Sea. This was a most difficult task. The timbers were frozen stiff, and trying to knock nails into them was nigh on impossible. The chippy, the one deck cadet on board and some of the crew, including me, laboured away at this grim task and eventually, after a week, it was done. It was then we noticed that the sugar did not come from Poland. Someone held up an empty bag and noticed the words 'Havana, Cuba' in the jute sacking. This was going to cause big problems later on, as the United States and Russia were about to throw rockets at each other over the missile crisis in Cuba.

When it was time to sail, another crisis arose. The wind had gone into the north and all the ice had piled up outside the harbour. We couldn't get out, so we had to wait – and wait we did for nearly three weeks, enjoying of course the delights of the Polana and other dives downtown.

Sailing at last, we broke out of the Baltic and took a pilot through the Kiel Canal and then out past Brunsbüttel and into the North Sea.

When we arrived in Middlesbrough we found that the heavy lift machinery had been cancelled. Somehow we were able to fill the holes in the middle of the hatches with suitable cargo, and eventually we sailed for Mombasa.

As we passed Gibraltar an American destroyer pulled abeam of us and demanded we stop while a search of the ship was carried out. The Welsh Git flatly refused. The destroyer followed us and was then joined by an even bigger warship, which pulled in on the opposite side. They said they intended to board us, but the Welsh Git again flatly refused. He said any attempt to get on board would be repulsed. I was wondering with what and by whom.

This cat-and-mouse game went on all the way to Port Said in Egypt, and when we tied up to the buoys in the harbour a delegation of officials from the British, American, French and German embassies came piling up the gangway. They were ensconced with the Welsh Git and the local agent for several hours.

We were carrying communist cargo and America did not like it. They were told in no uncertain terms to lump it as they could not stop free trade. Britain still had a bit of bottle in those days. The Yanks retired looking pretty peeved about the whole thing, and muttering about 'goddamn Limeys'.

Three weeks later we had finished discharging in Mombasa and were informed the ship was going to be sold, but first we were to go to Mozambique to load coal for Colombo.

We all streamed ashore in Mombasa for one last blast in the bars and byways of Kilindini Road. Returning to the dock in the early hours, at first we couldn't see the ship, but then Willy realized that all the lights were out. A blackout! Jesus had been 'flashing up' a boiler for sailing and he had misread the sight glass. The innards of the boiler had collapsed and he then had no power to get the donkey boiler going. Oh my! Woe is him!

At daylight it was decided to fire up another boiler with timber from the cargo holds, and the Nurnee and I spent all morning hurling planks down through the 'fiddly' to the engineers below. Many screams and shouts came up through the gratings as the large pieces of wood crashed down on the bottom plates. The old chief was none too pleased at the destruction of his engine room. By six in the evening, though, they had steam on another boiler, and by the morning the last two boilers were up and running. Our troubles did not end there, though: the ship could not sail without dispensation from a surveyor. One was tracked down, and as it was the fair-weather monsoon in the Indian Ocean he allowed us to sail.

Lourenço Marques in the 1960s was a lively town – an offshoot of Lisbon and Rio de Janeiro. There were plenty of bars and plenty of nightclubs, but there was one drawback. The ship was put on a coaling berth under a huge gantry. Thirty-ton rail wagons of coal were then hoisted up the gantry, and the whole thing tipped over so that the coal fell from a height of at least 60 feet into the ship. The dust and noise was indescribable. To make matters worse a huge wire spring was attached to either end of the ship, connected to a large steam winch under the gantry. This machinery was operated by an evil-looking Portuguese, and when the coal was piled up above the hatch tops he would engage the winch and the ship would move up and down the quay. This meant we had to be on continuous standby to tend the head and stern lines, and to keep the vessel from drifting off the berth. There was no shore leave for the deck officers. The coal dust was frightful. Attempts were made to seal the entrance doors and to protect the gyrocompass, but it was impossible. The dust got in everywhere.

There was no apartheid in Mozambique, but the Portuguese did not treat the local labour well. For a few extra cents coaling gangs were put down into the holds, each man with an Aladdin-style oil lamp. They then had to trim the coal back to the sides of the ship to get out of the lower holds through the small trimming hatches in the sides of the 'tween deck. If the oil lamp went out, they knew they were running out of air. These men were counted in and out by us. We did not want any corpses turning up in Colombo.

After over thirty-six hours of this hell we were loaded. The Portuguese would not let us wash the ship down. They did not want the harbour polluted.

At last we sailed, and started the long plod across the Indian Ocean to Colombo. The weather was fine, and the north-east monsoon held steady. The sea was like glass, and the sunrises and sunsets were spectacular. We even managed almost 14 knots on a couple of days.

Then one morning there was a large bang from down below, and the ship slowed to a stop. One of the engine-room crew had been working near the main circulating pump and dropped his spanner in it – truly a spanner in the works. It took nearly two days to fix.

Now another problem arose: the last two remaining boilers started to leak water in great quantities, and the ship started to run out of water to supply them. Five days from Colombo the engineers were forced to switch over to water from the deep tank – in other words, they had to use seawater. Our speed went down to about 6 knots and clouds of black oily smoke poured out of the funnel, some of it in great clumps which set the hatch covers alight on the after hatches.

At last we arrived off Colombo, and very quickly berthed, which was a surprise as there were about fifty ships outside waiting to dock. Ceylon, as it was then, was completely out of coal, so we had priority. Coal was discharged by what we called a 'dead man' swinging derrick into barges alongside. Such was the hurry to get the coal ashore that the time of twenty-one days laid down in the charter party was easily reached.

Water barges were continuously alongside, putting water on board for the boilers. During our spell there, the ship took on over 3,000 tons of fresh water. The mates were kept busy making sure the oil lamps in the hatches were kept primed and full of oil. We were in just as much hurry to get on our way as the Ceylonese were for the coal.

At last the nightmare was at an end. After giving thunderous blasts on our steam whistle to other Clan Line ships in the harbour, we sailed for Hong Kong and scrap.

Our passage across to the Malacca Strait was fine, and we now thought our troubles were over. Not so! We again ran out of fresh water for the boilers, and the old chief was forced to go back on to the salt tank. Slowly we passed through the strait, heading for Singapore for water. Oily smoke belched out of the funnel, covering the aft end of the ship in a gaseous cloud and forcing the crew to sleep on deck up forward.

As we neared Singapore a strange craft pulled in behind us. A shifty band of men were hiding beneath the gunwales. Strait pirates had latched on to us. Mercifully their craft was only a little faster than ours, and as they drew near we played fire hoses on them and threw anything handy at them. The Nurnee flashed into action and put out calls for help. Things were getting desperate when an Australian warship hove into view and drove the pirates off.

Our pilot in Singapore told us he sat on the veranda of the Raffles Hotel watching a cloud of black smoke coming round into Singapore, which he guessed was us.

After a quick run ashore in Bugie Street and other delights of the town, and having filled up with water for the boilers, we once more set off up the China Sea to Hong Kong.

This time we were lucky and arrived in one piece – just.

The pilots put us on a type-B buoy as we were expected to go to the scrapyard within days. The Bangladeshis were all paid off and all the heavy oil left in the ship was pumped ashore. There was a water crisis in Hong Kong and we had plenty of fresh water, so the ship was inundated with people coming on board for a shower.

Then the weather turned nasty. Typhoon Iris was rapidly approaching Hong Kong. The Port Authority demanded we put to sea, but we couldn't. We had no fuel and no crew. The old chief reckoned that with what we had we could steam for six hours, no more. The type-B buoy was not suitable for typhoons. The sale of the ship to the scrap firm was now delayed. The weather continued to get worse.

The Nurnee and I went ashore with Willy and Porteus for a run up the road in Kowloon. In the early hours it was blowing hard and we decided to go back to the ship, but the ferries had stopped running. We asked an American crew boat if they would take us back.

"Sure, pal, where is it?"

When we pointed out a dim light way down the harbour, he threw his engine into reverse and disappeared into the stormy night.

Eventually a police launch took us back. It was now blowing almost 90 knots, and streaming with rain. Plenty of water now.

A Greek vessel had dragged her moorings and came down on us. We tried everything to fend her off with old mattresses and tyres but all to no avail. The Johnny Greek slowly slid down our starboard side, ripping off rails and stanchions, and was then lost to view in the storm.

Somehow we lasted the night. With few supplies on board, we lived on steak from ashore for the next two days and then at last the sale was finalized. We left the ship and were taken to a hotel in Kowloon.

From Kai Tek Airport, we flew to London in a Comet. If we had known that three months later the same aircraft would crack up in the skies, maybe we would not have flown in it. As we lifted off the runway at Hong Kong I looked down. There was the old *Clan Brodie* below, but now lying right over on her side. She had finally given up. What an end to a once heroic ship with a story to tell!

The Comet stopped everywhere, including Bangkok; Dum Dum Airport in Calcutta (where the locals locked up Jesus because he was a South African – we stood outside the cell throwing peanuts at him); and Cairo. In Cairo an ugly old Arab with one eye came on board and proceeded to spray the aircraft from a 'flit gun' – I am sure it was camel pee. Whatever it was it certainly made us get out from the plane. The old boy most likely then had a good rummage to see if there was anything worth pinching.

As we flew onward towards London, the Nurnee and I found a nice area at the back and lay on two convenient boxes for a sleep. A stewardess fumed at us: "What do you think you are doing? Those are coffins with dead British servicemen inside." We hurried back to our seats.

And so we arrived in London. Another voyage, full of incident, was over. We all scattered to different parts of the country. Home at last! The *Clan Brodie* was now well scrapped. She had been a good sea ship and now she was possibly one of the first of the ships in the merchant service when ships really looked like ships to start the voyage to the graveyard. She was one of the greats.

At least now she didn't have a water problem any more.

LEGIONNAIRE

There she was, so low in the water that only her bridge and funnel were visible from the Rotterdam dockside. The heavy, sweet smell of crude oil permeated the wharf and the cargo pumps could be distinctly heard thumping and wheezing, sending the oil cargo ashore. The massive oil lines jumped and swayed as the oil flowed into the shoreside tanks.

None of us had been near an oil tanker in our seagoing lives, and the sight and sound of this smallish ship discharging cargo made us wonder if we had done the right thing by agreeing to sign on.

The appointment letter had arrived early one morning, and its contents took me aback somewhat: 'You have been appointed as Third Officer on the oil tanker *Scottish Ptarmigan* and you will serve a minimum of nine months.' A couple of sweeteners were then added: 'Double seniority will apply, and also East of Suez you will receive Nine Pounds on your monthly salary.'

My wife was none too pleased as we had been married less than two years. Somehow she was persuaded to accept the situation, but it was not a happy time.

So there we were – four new replacements standing on the dockside and wondering what on earth we had let ourselves in for.

The company was not a tanker company, and, arriving on board, we new ones found that none of the officers had really much idea how to operate the ship's cargo system.

She was under charter to British Petroleum. She could carry about 18,000 tons of cargo oils. Most of the officers lived amidships, and we were fortunate that an extra deck had been added during building and the cabins were large and spacious. The galley was down aft with all the Asian crew, and food was carried forward along the flying bridge at mealtimes in panniers slung Oriental-style over the stewards' shoulders. This essential duty was carried out in all weathers. Another flying bridge joined the midship section to the fo'c's'le.

The cargo was carried in a total of twenty-seven separate tanks – large, cavernous spaces entered by a small raised lid on the main deck. As crude oil gives off large amounts of vapour, this was passed through valves in each tank lid and then vented into the atmosphere from the top of the two masts. We soon found out that most of these relief valves, like much of the other equipment on board, did not work correctly.

Our destination was Bonny, in Nigeria, but before we loaded cargo all the tanks had to be washed out. In those days, the early 1960s, nobody gave a thought about pollution so our sludge water was pumped into a holding tank and then, once we were out in the ocean, over the side from the stern of the ship. This just does not happen today. All hands were involved in this work, even after doing a four-hour watch. There seemed to be little thought about personal safety, and many years were to pass before a serious attempt was made to make sure that the crew did not pass out and die after going into unventilated spaces.

We just ploughed on regardless, and one dark night in the Bay of Biscay one of the deck cadets and I were washing out tanks and topping up with seawater as ballast. The chief mate suddenly appeared when we had almost filled every tank and the seas were now thundering over the decks. We both got a rocket for attempting to submerge her completely.

A fascinating aspect of the small tankers of those days was the way they behaved in rough seas. With such a low freeboard when loaded, the decks were continually awash with water.

Waves broke right across the decks. It really was a most impressive if not frightening sight to see the whole forepart of the ship underwater with just the flying bridge and the tank lids showing above it.

The movement of the cargo and ballast water in the vessel was controlled by two large pump rooms, one forward and one aft. An Indian pump man was employed, and he appeared to know more about the system than the officers overseeing him.

In Bonny we realized how dangerous life could be on an oil tanker – especially one like the *Scottish Ptarmigan*. Crude oil was pumped into the ship from the tank farm ashore, generally at a rate of 2,000 tons per hour. Because of our poor pumping lines and tank valve system we usually reduced this by a third, but it was still pretty fast.

The most dangerous part of the loading occurred as the cargo was nearly all aboard. The rate was reduced to about 500 tons per hour and the process of 'topping off' the tanks could then be carried out. This was done by measuring the depth from the top of the tank to the oil with a large wooden dipstick. These heights had been pre-calculated. The last tank to 'top off' was usually a centre tank near to the cargo control room, the rate then being reduced to about 200 tons per hour.

We soon found that because of the poor state of the tank top relief valves, the big lids on the tank top had to be cracked open to relieve the pressure. Raw crude-oil gas then spilled out over the decks. One spark and we would have been goners.

The loading process involved all the deck officers and cadets, and many a frantic and panic-stricken time we had 'topping her off'.

The heat, the flies and the bugs in Bonny were grim to say the least, and after sailing we collapsed asleep if we were not on watch. It made us wonder why we did not get a bonus for working in West Africa.

No thought was given by the owners to changing the articles

of agreement. We had signed a two-year set of articles and therefore could expect no change whilst on the *Ptarmigan*.

It took two days to discharge the cargo in Finnart in Scotland, then off to the Middle East we went. Heavy seas in the Bay of Biscay and the Mediterranean made working out on deck difficult, and we all became very adept at jumping to safety during tank-cleaning.

The ship cleared Suez and our bonus payments started. Mind you, £2-odd was deducted for tax. We all settled down to the boring routine of life on board a tanker. Films were shown, supplied from a library ashore, and we played endless games of cards and Monopoly.

Our first cargo was loaded in Mina al Ahmadi in Kuwait for Kwinana in Western Australia. The voyage took us out of the Persian Gulf down to the southern end of India then across the Indian Ocean to Fremantle. The ship did six of these voyages on the trot, and it became so monotonous that after two of them the cadets would take the watches during the day and the second mate and I would just do the navigation and then sleep or something.

The sparky had a canary called Joey. This little fellow would wander about and visit everybody. He loved a few drops of Drambuie, and after a drink he would fall asleep with his legs in the air. The sparky had to declare Joey to Australian Customs and Immigration and a bond of £50 was put on the little chap, the sparky being the guarantor.

During one voyage, passing India, two large black crows came on board and lodged themselves behind the funnel. Passing the Lombok Strait, another ship hove into view heading east, and the crows flew off towards it looking for a better feeding ground than ours. Crows cannot fly very far, and they soon returned exhausted. Squawking angrily, they settled down again behind the funnel.

During that passage to Kwinana we heard the news of President Kennedy's assassination, and for days we huddled around our radio sets picking up every scrap of information from the BBC.

As we neared Fremantle, the Captain made the mistake of declaring the two crows to the authorities. The ship was ordered to anchor in the quarantine anchorage in Cockburn Sound, and a boat approached with a posse of men and customs officials all armed with shotguns. They streamed up the gangway ladder, and one of them running down aft let fly two rounds from his twelve-bore. We nearly died with fright.

"Do you want to blow us all up? This is an oil tanker," the mate shouted, with a few choice swear words thrown in.

The crows meanwhile took off and were last seen doing a bombing run into the Australian outback. The Aussies were not pleased, and we spent a further day at anchor while it was all sorted out and fines were paid.

Unfortunately we were to get into more trouble with Aussie customs. A few voyages later we loaded diesel oil in Kwinana for Whyalla in the Spencer Gulf, then Melbourne and finally Napier in New Zealand.

Whyalla was an ore terminal, there being huge deposits of iron ore in the area. Our magnetic compasses went haywire as we proceeded up the Spencer Gulf. It was exceedingly hot and dry.

It was during the trip up the Spencer Gulf that disaster struck. Joey, with a skinful of Drambuie inside him, was sucked out of the entrance door at the end of the alleyway. He went over the side and was manfully flying along with the ship. A couple of times he almost made it into one of the lifeboats, but a huge gannet swooped down, there was a cloud of feathers and little Joey was no more.

The immigration people in Whyalla went into convulsions. A most heinous crime had been committed and we were accused of bringing all kinds of horrible diseases into Australia. After a dozen of us had signed a document witnessing his demise the ship got away with it. The sparky lost his £50.

Two days were spent offloading diesel oil, then we sailed on round to Melbourne. This was the first civilized port we had seen in months, and the officers on duty kept shutting the steam valves back on the cargo pumps to lengthen the ship's stay in port.

Then we travelled on across the Tasman Sea to Napier to discharge the remaining cargo. Tying the ship up alongside in Napier was a tiresome business. Large wire cables had to be hauled on board fore and aft. The cables were attached to lengths of very thick coir rope, which were slipped over the bollards on the dock. These were in addition to our own mooring lines. The dock was exposed to the Southern Ocean swell, and the ships could range twenty feet or more up and down the quayside. On one occasion a tug had to be ordered to hold us alongside. The movement was so great that we were in danger of breaking the oil line to the quay.

Apart from that most of us were able to enjoy a short run up the road, and we made ready use of the bars and byways, but, as in Australia, the 'five o'clock swill' was in force. The pubs only opened for one hour and shut at six o'clock. Vast amounts of beer were consumed in that one hour, and at closing time the town was filled with drunken and brawling men. It was several years before both countries got rid of the 'swill' and had proper opening hours until ten in the evening.

From Napier we headed off south of New Zealand back to Kwinana. The passage from Stewart Island (the most southerly point in that part of the ocean) was horrendous. It was wintertime and the seas (travelling around the world with nothing to stop them) gave us a terrible beating. We had much more ballast water than usual in the tanks to ease the movement of the ship, but the rolling became so bad we lost the gyrocompass. The second mate and I tried to fix it, and bits of gyro were lying all over the wheelhouse deck, but it was no good. We staggered along south of Australia using the magnetic compass, and we had to keep the ship in 'hand steering' as the autopilot was out.

Then came a surprise. Our next cargo was another lot of diesel oil, this time for Kobe in Japan. To a certain extent this cheered us up a bit, as at least we were not going into the Persian Gulf. But it was wintertime in Japan, and the passage northwards was extremely rough. It now felt as though we were sailing on a submarine, the decks never being free of solid water. The temperature of the oil in the tanks had to be maintained at about 80 degrees by heating coils in the tanks, and the cadets and sailors had to go out on deck in stormy weather to do daily checks. With harnesses on and lashed to the railings and ladders, they quite often disappeared completely under the water. It was a worrying time for everybody.

Kobe proved exceptionally cold. Japan had not really got into its full stride after the war, and there was much poverty. The exchange rate was over 1,000 yen to the pound, and we made hay whilst the sun shone. Before not many years had passed, 200 yen to the pound would be a good deal.

My experiences when a cadet at bumming drinks stood me in good stead, and we always headed for bars with plenty of American servicemen in them. They were good chaps and felt sorry for us and kept us well supplied with beers. The ship stayed almost three days in Kobe, and we were sorry to see Japan falling astern as we headed south once more towards Mina and the Persian Gulf. Maybe this time we would get a cargo for Europe and 'Land's End for orders'. We did not know it then, but we had an awful long way to go yet.

Pulling off the dock in Mina, we received orders to proceed to Karachi. So that was why we had loaded maximum cargo in the tanks! No Atlantic this trip! The gloom on board deepened. The second mate now had a child seven months old and he, more than anyone, was longing for home. Things were to get worse as we did three runs to and from Karachi.

Our first call there was nearly our last. Discharge was slow, the lines on the shore not being very large. The locals all took to sleeping underneath the pipes on the dockside, and many times we had to go down and stop them lighting fires for cooking. Only about 200 tons of cargo was left in one tank, but it was proving impossible to pump out. The small 'stripping pump' was put on it, but even that proved ineffective. Steam was then introduced into the tank to try to force the oil out, but it was no good. The chief mate then gave orders to put compressed air into the tank and bring it up to 7 bars (7 pounds per square inch). The oil started to flow. The lines on the quay started to lift and make knocking noises. The labour underneath ran away towards town clutching their lungis around them. A BP representative appeared and asked what we were doing. When it was explained to him what was happening he went very pale.

"You silly buggers! One spark and you will blow Karachi Harbour off the map. Never put air into an unwashed and non-gas-free tank," he explained.

Apparently compressed air builds up static in the tanks.

As he shot off down the gangway, his last instruction was to let the air out very, very slowly. We knew he was worried as we could see some fire engines and an ambulance parked up behind a shed.

We did not do that again.

Then we sailed to Mina again and took on a cargo of diesel oil, not for the Far East, but for Djibouti in French Somalia. The Gulf of Aden is hot, but Djibouti is even hotter. It was so hot there that boots had to be worn on deck, as ordinary shoes would burn our feet. The place was still in the hands of the French, and the local people would drive up and down the road near the docks every evening in an attempt to get cool.

The cargo took an age to discharge, so a posse of us went up the road and found some very busy bars in the main drag. After a few beers we struck up a conversation with some French Foreign Legion soldiers. Most of them were Germans, and you did not have to be an expert to know what they had been up to in the last war.

We became friendly with an English legionnaire, and he asked me if I would like to go on patrol with him and his men the next morning. So, after getting permission from the mate, the senior cadet and I waited outside the dock gate very early the next day. The legion arrived in what looked like an upturned bathtub on wheels, with gun ports cut into the sides and a manhole on top of it, down which we dropped. There were wooden seats inside, no cushions, and of course it was unbearably hot.

We drove off into the desert, where there was nothing much to see except scrub and thorn trees and the odd Somali with a droopy-looking camel. Mercifully we had brought water with us, as by ten in the morning it was almost unbearable in our metal coffin. The legionnaires just sat and grinned at us. They were a hardbitten lot. Several hours passed and then we came upon an encampment where many Somalis were gathered round cooking fires. Several camels and goats were tethered to the thorn trees. We gratefully got out of our travelling box. Food was offered – I think it must have been rice and goat. It looked and tasted very greasy. Then – surprise, surprise! – behind a thorn tree and connected to a small generator was a fridge, and ice-cold Cokes were produced. What relief!

When we headed back towards Djibouti in our coffin my shirt was plastered to my back; the three-hour return trip was extremely painful. I am sure the Germans in the patrol were getting their own back for coming second in the war.

On the outskirts of Djibouti we pulled up at a farmhouse. The owner was a German. He ran a small zoo and also a bar, and he produced bottles of ice-cold lager. To see the beer slowly spilling down the side of the glass and the condensation on the outside was like seeing manna from heaven. We downed several.

After parting from our legion friends we arrived back on board and met a party going ashore. The cargo operations had stopped for the night, so we joined them. We all went to a bar in Djibouti, where I knocked back more cold lagers. The legionnaires arrived, and we drank more beers together. It started to turn into a long night.

Now, one thing a legionnaire values more than his life is his kepi. I managed to lift a bright-red one off the bar and head down the road towards the ship wearing it. It would have made a fine memento to take home. I did not get far.

"*Schweinehund*, that's my hat!"

A large German sergeant pinned me to the road and removed his kepi from my head.

That concluded our stay in Djibouti. The next morning, the combination of the heat and too many cold Amstels meant I had a hangover to beat all hangovers. To this day I can still feel the hammers going off in my brain. I did not drink Amstel beer again for a long time.

After two more trips from Mina to Djibouti, we thought, 'This is it. The next cargo will be Land's End.'

No such luck! As we pulled once more off the berth, we were told that our destination was Kwinana. Despondency descended. The second mate became extremely reclusive. He had been on board for ten months. The experience eventually became too much for him, and on our eventual return to England he resigned from the company.

Another six weeks passed. We had returned to Mina, and this time as we left the dock we were told we were bound for Land's End at last. The gloom lifted, and we joyfully pointed the ship's bows towards Suez and home.

Forty-eight hours before arriving off Land's End we all advised the Captain that we wished to pay off in the first British port. This was our legal right.

After docking in the Isle of Sheppey we waited the arrival of the company rep with reliefs and our pay off in wages. We had been away eleven months and steamed 100,000 miles. We had only been in port thirty-three days, of which we had only sixteen with access to the shore. Everyone was more than ready to go home.

The company man arrived, and we were asked to take the ship to Sweden and then pay off in Newcastle, maybe.

There was a flat refusal from all hands – except the chief mate, who was hoping for command. It was then found that the Captain had not forwarded the request for reliefs. The ship was delayed and the owners frantically searched for officers to take the ship onwards. We left the berth and anchored in the stream.

At last our reliefs appeared and came up the gangway. They told us that none of them had ever sailed on a tanker before. Now, there was an interesting bit of news – neither had we.

As we went down the gangway, none of us looked back at the *Ptarmigan*. There are some voyages you just want to forget.

When I arrived home my wife recognized me, and the next morning after breakfast she advised me there was no money in the bank. The London office had conveniently forgotten to pay my wages in for two months – just another wrinkle of life working on oil tankers!

DR YES

We sailed just after Christmas. It was midwinter, with gales and rain. We were carrying 500 passengers on a cruise to the Canary Islands. The ship had already done one trip down there, and most of the 'bloods', as we called them, were sailing again for another go. I do not think they realized what they were in for this time.

The ship had been especially converted to one class from the normal first and tourist classes, and by clever marketing the owners had filled the ship for both trips.

Ronnie Carroll, the singer, along with a lady called Yana, would entertain in the evenings; the only problem with that was Mr Carroll was not often sober. Yana, a very beautiful woman, preferred the female sex and carried quite an entourage of hangers-on with her.

But away we went, down the Solent and past Calshot Spit with one of the Queen Elizabeth flying boats parked up in mothballs on the foreshore. Dropping the pilot at the Needles, we headed off down-Channel into the teeth of a force-eight gale.

The next morning the ship was labouring heavily in rough seas and a mounting swell. Speed was cut back, and the crew rigged the safety ropes in the passenger corridors. Most of the 'bloods' were hardened travellers and very few were sick, but by the next day we were out in the Atlantic in storm conditions and mountainous seas. The Captain was a very indifferent character and relied completely on his officers, all of whom were professionals, both deck and engine. The man himself was incapable of making decisions.

I was on the midnight-to-four watch, and by three o'clock in the morning I turned the huge vessel head to sea to minimize the violent rolling. We stayed on a westerly course all day, and then tried turning her to run south with the weather behind us. Hopefully to clear Cape Finisterre. The seas were so large that the wave behind us reared up higher than the stern and the back of the previous wave reared up ahead of us nearly 700 feet away.

Below decks, though, the partying went on. I would go down early in the morning and drink black velvet, Guinness and champagne with Ronnie and Yana and a very wealthy London dentist. The other passengers also seemed to enjoy the atrocious conditions. We were all young and full of the Swinging Sixties enthusiasm. A storm in the Bay of Biscay was a mere bagatelle.

On New Year's Eve we were still in heavy weather. At sea the youngest person on the ship rings sixteen bells at midnight, and one of the young deck boys was primed up for this job. Unfortunately one of the Scottish junior engineers appeared at five minutes to the hour, drunk and completely naked, and rang the bells. He was chased around the passenger lounge by an assortment of masters-at-arms and various officers and was eventually subdued and carried away kicking and screaming. The 'bloods' thought it was all very funny and part of the entertainment.

I went up on watch and found the ship now running down the Portuguese coast but still in very rough seas. She was rolling anything up to 45 degrees each way, which made life all over the ship difficult. Everything was sliding and crashing about, and the mess in the galleys and storerooms was horrific.

After coming off watch I turned in, and wedged myself into my bunk with extra pillows and cushions, hoping to get some sleep. An hour later I was awake with excruciating pain in my lower back, and being sick with it. I managed to crawl out into the wheelhouse and I rolled across the deck under the mate's feet. He thought I was drunk, but quickly realized I was in agony.

The Doctor was called on the telephone, and two burly able seamen picked me up and carried me down nine flights of stairs to the sickbay.

The Doctor was newly qualified at Guy's Hospital in London, and before taking up a practice he thought he would try this seafaring thing, having been quite impressed with the film *Doctor at Sea*. He was a terribly efficient little sod, and seasickness had made him even more diabolically efficient. Now here was the little second mate rolling around in agony on the surgery floor.

"Right," he said to me, "I must make a thorough examination."

"Never mind that, Doc," I managed to say. "Just give me something quick."

Dr Yes, as we called him, was having none of it. He proceeded to go through an examination, which took him about ten minutes. I was now at the point of no return and pleading with him for help. His nurse looked on with amusement. She was what we called a 'hardened bitch', having spent three years working on the Snowy River Scheme in Australia.

"I must just check your prostate gland. It won't take long," said he, pulling on a rubber glove.

He had just made contact when the ship gave an almighty roll and he and I flew through the air with his finger still inserted to land on the opposite bulkhead, which was now the floor. The ship then rolled back the other way and we crashed across the other side of the room.

"Did that hurt?" he asked.

"No," I replied. "Do it again."

I was now in extremis with pain, but my sense of humour shone threw it all.

"Oh, you bloody sailors are all the same."

Dr Yes had met his match.

Three days later I was up and running again after a severe bout of kidney stones – but I never drank black velvet again.

Note: Passengers, 'pax' or 'bloods' were given that name as the sole occupation of the crew in those days was to extract money from them by whatever means possible – bleed them. Most of the stewards and barmen were the wealthiest men afloat, but they all gave excellent service.

BAR MARITIMO

She was the first of the modern-day cruise liners, leading the way in the operation of carrying large numbers of passengers cruising-style, feeding and entertaining them for ten days or more, and then changing them over for a fresh lot at the end of a voyage inside twelve hours. We would dock in the morning and sail the same evening.

She had started life trading to South America and the Caribbean, carrying cargo, mails and passengers, and now she was permanently on bareboat charter to the Union Castle Line, sailing on ten- and fourteen-day cruises out of Southampton.

The four cargo holds had all been gutted, and the spaces filled with cabins; the main deck areas had been modified and extra lounges and bars fitted. One thousand passengers could now be carried. The ship's main bar was the longest then afloat and the lounge could seat 600 people. It was said that when she carried more than 700 passengers, the ship was making a profit. She became immensely popular with the travelling public. Entertainment on board was of a very high standard, and a cruise director was appointed to manage it all.

The downside was the on-board safety. The watertight integrity of the cargo holds could not be breached with additional doors and walkways (there was not going to be another situation like on the *Titanic*, where the water flowed over the tops of the bulkheads into the next space), so access to the cabins was up and down flights of stairs over the tops of the bulkheads at main deck level.

This proved to be a nightmare as far as fire watches were concerned, particularly at night, and two groups of seamen were on duty, one at the forepart of the ship and the other aft. The ship's officers and crew were continually having to be exercised at fire and emergency drills.

She was a happy ship and went to many exciting places. In the winter months, in an attempt to capture the South African market, cruises across the South Atlantic to South America were tried. They were only partially successful because of the great distance involved, and it was not always possible to fill the ship from South Africa.

There were many well-known characters on board amongst the officers and crew. One young man serving as a steward decided to take photographs and sell them to the passengers. This proved so popular that he ended up as the official ship's photographer, selling black-and-white prints to the passengers at £1 each. Every time they moved, snap! Going ashore, drinking in bars, playing games on deck . . . there he was with his team. For the 'bloods' there was no escape. Needless to say, his business was very profitable.

The ship's laundry was run by a hidden band of Chinese. Down in the bowels of the ship they laboured away for hours, handling the enormous amount of linen and towels, which needed constant attention. Many were the arguments between the head laundryman and officers who lost shirts and white uniforms in this hellhole. The head laundryman would sit cross-legged on a table and was immune to all entreaties as to missing laundry.

"No savvy. No see. Maybe next week you luckee."

Complaints to the senior catering officers and staff had no effect. The Chinese laundry ploughed on with remorseless inefficiency.

I had been appointed as the senior navigating officer of this fine vessel, and a most interesting job it was too. I was not only doing the day-to-day navigation of the vessel, but I was also planning and plotting the cruises maybe two years ahead. The results of these plans were sent to Head Office in London for approval. On one occasion, planning a cruise to ports in the Baltic, Head Office advised that their plan for one section of the voyage was some six hours shorter than the one I had presented. When it was pointed out that the ship had to steam out and round the still considerable number of minefields in existence in the North Sea and the Baltic Sea, a deafening silence came from the powers that lived and worked in Leadenhall Street.

The little Welsh captain informed me, "You've got them there, boyo."

But of course everything was not all plain sailing. One voyage, after a dry-docking, we set off across the Bay of Biscay for the Canary Islands. A new chief officer had been appointed, and he was of the opinion that the ship would go faster for the same amount of fuel if she was about a foot down by the head. He gave orders for the engineers and carpenters to pump about 200 tons of ballast water into the double bottom below No. 1 Hatch. This space was used as a storeroom for all types of gear needed to keep the ship clean and operational – everything from toilet paper and soap to buckets and brooms.

I arrived for my watch at four o'clock in the morning as we heaved along across the ocean at 18-odd knots and remarked to the other second officer I was relieving, "She feels a bit heavy for'ard."

"No, old boy, it's your imagination," he replied as he left the wheelhouse.

My worries were confirmed just after five in the morning when a very frightened-looking deck boy appeared at the wheelhouse door blabbing on in a fine Glaswegian accent: "See youse, theys watter coming up oot o' the hatch wey the stores in it, Jimmie."

When we had calmed him down it was established that the lower alleyways in the forepart of the ship were flooding.

The junior officer on watch was dispatched below with one of the sailors, and he very shortly reported that the hatch was full of seawater, and it was coming up into the cabins on the bottom deck.

I rang the engine room and asked them if they were moving any ballast.

Another Scottish voice replied, "Och aye, we've been

transferring water since eight last night, Jimmy. Naebody has told us to stop pumping."

"Well, stop it," I ordered.

I called out the chief officer and the carpenter. All the stores in the hatch were ruined and several cabins had water inside them. The passengers within were asleep and oblivious to the danger. Once the water had been removed by portable pump, it was found that the manhole lids to the double bottoms had not been bolted tightly down after the ship's stay in dry dock, though the record book was signed up to say they had been.

The chief officer and the carpenter left at the end of that voyage.

And so we cruised on to all ports in the Mediterranean, the Canary Islands and the Baltic Sea. One of the most popular ports was Lisbon, and the ship called there regularly. To maintain the Lisbon call the Portuguese asked for and got at least two calls to the Azores during our summer cruising schedule. We did one trip in July and it blew a westerly gale for a week. Hundreds of our passengers were seasick, and people were lying about all over the upper decks. The toilets were in constant use.

We arrived back in Lisbon, that voyage, to a big civic function laid on by the authorities with plenty of local singers and dancers to entertain the sea-weary people. The ship came grandly alongside the quay, where the Portuguese had military bands thumping away on the dockside. The bandsmen were all decked out in colourful uniforms, banging away on drums and puffing bravely on huge tubas and trombones, giving plenty of oompah. A large group of dignitaries and their ladies were gathered in grand style on a flag-bedecked dais, and the little Welsh captain with company officials went along to greet them. Passengers crowded the rails and streamers flew back and forth. The bugles blew, the drums rolled and there was much oompahing from the tubas as the ceremony reached a climax. Suddenly two stray pie-dogs, scruffy-looking individuals, trotted out from the cargo shed and started to mate frantically, directly in front of the officials on the platform.

Cheers went up from the gathered throng on board the ship, there were blushes from all the ladies, gasps from the local gentry and cries of "Go, doggy, go!" from the crew. Fat policemen waddled down the dock in a vain attempt to drive the coupling pair off. More howls of derision came from the passengers and sailors peering over the ship's side. One of the cooks appeared with a bucket of water and doused the pair to delirious cheers from the onlookers.

Order was eventually restored and we all retired to the bar for a well-earned drink. That voyage went down as the 'Shaggy Dog Trip'.

Our next voyage came to be known as 'Dicing with Jesus'. We had a new relief captain, a large, imposing man. He came from the very north of Scotland and was completely teetotal and also, as we all said, 'married to the Lord'. His party piece with the passengers was giving a sermon on Sunday mornings at the church parade. This was held in the cinema. We officers would be dished out with marked £5 and £10 notes, and these would be produced with a flourish when the collection plate went round, the idea being to encourage the 'bloods' to dig deep. The new captain did not approve of this method of raising extra cash.

One Sunday morning we were all in the cinema with the muffled peal of church bells coming out over the Tannoy system. All seats were taken – about 300 people waiting to listen to the Captain's sermon. I read a lesson, gazing up into the gods, where some attractive young women were sitting, and then it was sermon time.

Striding manfully on to the stage, the Captain took his place behind the lectern. In a deep, powerful voice, with his blue eyes flashing, he proceeded to preach to the congregation. He was well into his stride when a ship's whistle sounded from almost right ahead, one long blast. He paused and then went on in fine style. Another blast came, this time from the whistle right above us in the funnel. Oh dear, perhaps we were in fog, and there was a ship ahead of us. Two minutes later the first whistle sounded again, from right ahead of us. In full stride, the Captain's features went white. Now he was in trouble: he couldn't leave and hurry to the bridge, because that would have alarmed the travelling public. In stumbling tones he continued. God was getting a pasting.

The chief officer looked at me and I slipped out of a side door and legged it as quickly as I could up to the wheelhouse. The ship was sailing in brilliant clear weather. A newly qualified third mate was on watch. He was a Royal Naval Reserve officer, and full of it.

"What's going on?" I demanded.

"Oh, I thought I would test the whistles," he said in a plummy voice. "Did I do wrong?"

"Yes, you bloody fool, you did."

The whistles were stopped from sounding off, and I returned to the cinema. The Captain was sitting at the back of the stage looking decidedly uncomfortable. The chief officer had taken over the service. My thumbs-up sign didn't seem to help matters.

Our brush with God did not end there. Two days later we arrived off the port of Palma in Majorca. The Captain had now regained his confidence and he approached the breakwaters and pilot station at full speed. A large American aircraft carrier was anchored within half a mile of the outer mole, and it was right in our line of approach. The ship maintained its course and its fast speed of about 12 knots. The carrier was now very close, and groups of American sailors started to gather on her flight deck. There was very little space between the breakwater and the warship. The pilot on his boat started to scream at us in Spanish over the VHF. Sailors on the carrier were now jumping up and down and waving their arms at us, frantically trying to wave us off. We were now going to pass within about fifty feet of her side. The air was frantic with whistles blowing and voices coming over the VHF screaming at us to "Get your arse out of here!"

I went up to the Captain, who appeared oblivious to the fuss.

"We are a bit close to the Ham Shank, sir."

"I know, I know, but God is with us."

We shot down the carrier's port side. I could see the looks of alarm on the faces of the American sailors. What the Japanese dive-bombers couldn't do in the war we could achieve in less than a minute. Our helm went over hard a-port as we approached the harbour, the pilot managed to get on board, and the engines were put full astern. She was brought up short a few feet away from the dock ahead.

The helmsman, a wily old salt, came out with "Christ, he did that without a drink in him!"

We officers retired below to pray over a gin bottle.

The small Welsh captain returned from leave.

"I like you, boyo," he said to me. "You are the only one I don't have to look up at."

Around this time our fortunes started to take a bit of a nosedive. There were undercurrents amongst the British crew about the continued employment of Spanish stewards in the dining rooms. The Spanish made excellent waiters, and were cheerful and hard-working; our own stewards were generally good but prone to drunkenness. The National Union of Seamen did not help matters by threatening industrial action if the Spanish were not removed from the ship.

The vessel's next call was at Cadiz. This port was a maze of narrow streets and there were plenty of small bars. The main tipple was sherry, which was produced just up the road in Jerez. Our crew went ashore and proceeded to do the British thing in many of these bars. It was unfortunate that the Captain stepped into one of these places to be confronted by a somewhat drunken crowd of British sailors. There was considerable pushing and shoving and cries of "Welsh Git!" and the little man was removed into the street. In the process he lost his false teeth, and back on board he retired to his cabin just behind the wheelhouse, not to be seen by anybody but the most senior officers.

We sailed from Cadiz with the Captain incarcerated in his cabin.

The next morning was church parade. Another chief officer was appointed to officiate, and again he was a bit of a dud. He was not popular with the senior officers on board, and there were many arguments. The Captain delegated me to read the lesson.

On my table in the main dining room I had a family from Glasgow – five of them, mother and four daughters, none very attractive. They would all add to every sentence the word 'seemingly' – for example, "Seemingly, it will be a fine day today." I nicknamed them the Seeminglys.

My mistake was informing them that I would be reading the lesson at church the following morning.

"Seemingly, we never go to the kirk, but this time we will, to see youse."

The following morning things were not going well. We officers were in the chief officer's cabin drinking gin and tonic. He was nervous. I asked him what lesson he wanted me to read.

"It's up to you," he said. "Choose what you like."

A deck boy appeared in the doorway.

"There are no hymn books," he said.

"They are in the locker on the stage," I told him.

"I know, but where's the key?"

The chief electrician had the key as the film equipment was kept in there, but he and the chief mate had fallen out and there was no sign of him or his key.

With ten minutes to go, the master-at-arms appeared and asked the chief officer if he wanted to cancel the parade as there were no hymn books. No decision was being made, and the mate was in a funk.

I slipped out of the door, and grabbed hold of the deck boy. I handed him a fire axe and told him to open the locker door with it. Another mistake!

Instead of just prising the locker open, the young man ran across the stage and started to hammer frantically at the door with the axe, much to the amusement of the gathered throng. The bells were now pealing, and they combined with the hammering on the door. The audience started to chant, "Why are we waiting?"

The books fell out across the stage and were quickly gathered up and distributed through the cinema. The master-at-arms, a Korean VC, informed the chief officer that the parade could start. We officers, headed by the mate, all in our starched white uniforms, paraded down and on to the stage.

Nervously the mate started the service. He mumbled on. Looking down at the female officers in the front row, I noticed that many of them were trying not to laugh, and some were pointing at me in a frantic sort of way. Looking down, I saw that my white trousers had split from the knee to the crutch, and all was exposed. The Seeminglys, up in the gods, were falling around with laughter. I tried to cover my distress. It was now my turn to read the lesson.

Standing up, I read the first line of the shortest sentence in the Bible: "Jesus wept."

It was said in such a tone that the whole congregation erupted in gales of laughter. The service was terminated and we escaped, again to a bar to console ourselves.

Of course the complaints rolled in. The Seeminglys told me at dinner that it was better than any of the shows put on at night. We were all lucky not to be fired, though the chief mate was removed on the ship's return to Southampton. The Captain remained hidden in his cabin.

A day or two later we again arrived off the port of Palma. There was no aircraft carrier in our way this time, but there was one lying alongside the quay behind our berth with a couple of cruisers and a submarine. The American 6th Fleet was in port.

It was my turn to be stay-on-board duty officer, looking after the ship and generally having a quiet time of it. The other officers made the most of their day off in port. My time was spent working in the wheelhouse on charts and navigational problems, and at 'crew smoke O' I stepped out on to the wing of the bridge with a cup of coffee. Two of the ship's female staff joined me. The dockside was full of American sailors streaming ashore off the warships. Directly opposite the ship was the Ocean Terminal, with the large Bar Maritimo on its upper level. Many of our crew were already in there knocking back Cerveza and coffee solos. They were soon joined by large numbers of American sailors, whose ships were dry, and a good old party got going.

After about an hour there was much pushing and shoving going on between them all, then tables and chairs came flying out through the windows, and the crowd inside swirled round punching and kicking. The fighting spilled out on to the balcony and down the stairs. More Americans started running along the dock from their ships, and young male passengers and more of our sailors swarmed down the gangways and joined in.

Whistles blew and the Guardia Civil appeared, only to be beaten back with their funny hats all askew. Military police from the naval ships now appeared and starting laying about with their nightsticks. There must have now been over 200 people milling about and fighting on the quayside. With sirens blaring, large lorries appeared and Spain's special police arrived – jackbooted riot squads, who proceeded to lay into all and sundry with considerable ferocity.

The little Welsh captain appeared next to me on the bridge wing minus his teeth.

"What are they doin'?" he enquired.

"Fighting, sir," I told him.

"Well, go down and stop it."

There was not much I could do. The authorities were not pleased – an 'international incident' they called it.

Two tugs appeared and we were moved 'dead ship' to the outer mole and banned from ever going alongside the Ocean Terminal again. Coaches then had to be organized to get returning passengers out to the ship's berth – a distance of about 2 miles. No doubt the Americans were also in bad odour with the Spanish.

The other officers returned.

"What you been doin', then?" they asked.

"Not a lot," I said; "just cementing Anglo-American relations."

We retired to a quiet bar on board for another drink.

WEE GEORGIE

The years immediately after the Second World War saw a rapid expansion of the British merchant navy. By the 1960s almost 150,000 people were employed on British ships. Some 45,000 were officers; the remainder were ratings in deck, engine and catering departments.

Many of the shipping lines employed Asian seamen, from India, Pakistan, Bangladesh and China.

British-born sailors varied from the excellent to the downright awful. If a ship was sailing in a hurry and was short-handed, she had to take on anything the local shipping pool had to offer, and quite often these proved to be a bad lot.

The ratings working on the large passenger liners were in the main above average, and many of the stewards in particular gave valuable service. There was always a fair sprinkling of gays amongst the stewards, employed mainly because they did not bother the female passengers.

In the large mail ships sailing to South Africa, the crew would hold a concert maybe twice a year in the crew bar or 'pig'. These concerts were on a par with shows at the London Palladium, and many well-known names worked on the ships before they became famous. Russ Conway was one. Living conditions for men on board were not that great. Quite often there were six or more to a cabin, and they often worked from five o'clock in the morning until late at night. On ships the quiet period was from one o'clock to half past three in the afternoon, and basically everybody got their head down during this time. A first-class topside steward working in the passenger lounges would quite often be still hard at it at two in the morning.

There were many characters amongst this polyglot assortment of men – and some women – but one I recall with some amusement, and also a lot of horror, was a small Glaswegian man called, funnily enough, Wee Georgie Woods.

I first met him on a ship sailing from London. It was a week away from Christmas and we were short-handed for deck and catering ratings. The local agents were scouring the bars and byways of the East India Dock Road, and within an hour of the ship sailing hauled on board a bedraggled-looking bunch of men they had dragged out of local pubs. There was a sprinkling of deckies and stewards. The deckies turned out to be a bad bunch, but amongst the stewards was Wee Georgie.

He signed on blind drunk, with just a small bag of possessions and a pair of shoes. He was put in charge of the chief catering officer, kitted out with a steward's uniform and put to bed.

We sailed for East Africa. We had the usual rough passage across the Bay of Biscay and down into the Mediterranean, and it was only when we got into some fine weather that I first noticed the antics of Wee Georgie.

He had been put to serve on a large table of ten persons – a table nicknamed by the stewards an 'aircraft carrier'. There were several Egyptian passengers on this table and the table manners were very base. They continually shouted at Georgie and spread their food about all over the table. Georgie would appear, usually being well endowed with drink, and plunk the plates down in front of this lot.

One lunchtime, Georgie had obviously partaken of a hefty number of beers in the pig, and he appeared through the galley doors weaving his way unsteadily to the table. His nose was flushed a bright red, and he was mouthing obscenities in his sharp Glaswegian accent. The senior Egyptian, a doctor travelling home with his family, started to shout at the steward. Georgie faced up to him.

"Youse want soup, youse Gyppo git? Well, try this for size, Jimmy."

He promptly poured the soup neatly into the Doctor's lap.

"An' have some rice wi' it," he added, emptying a large jorum of rice over his head.

The Egyptian party fell on Wee Georgie, kicking and biting. Georgie appeared from under the melee, landing punches left and right.

The catering officer moved in quickly and dragged him kicking and screaming into the galley.

We officers sat at our table wishing for a bit more of the fun to develop, but the situation was calmed down, and the well-splattered doctor was removed to clean himself up.

The next morning at eleven sharp Georgie was marched into the Captain's cabin to receive his punishment. He was still worse the wear for drink, and he was hanging between the shoulders of two masters-at-arms, who had brought him along.

"What have you got to say for yourself?" demanded the Captain.

"Gi' me half a chance and I'll din the bugger agin," retorted the wee man.

"I fine you four days' pay for violent behaviour. You are banned from the saloon and will work in the galley on general cleaning duties," intoned the Captain.

"Up yours, Cap'n!"

The Captain shooed him out of his room. He could not fine him any more for that offence, but it was pretty obvious Georgie would be back.

Sure enough, during the next few weeks he made regular appearances at a logging session, for being either drunk on duty or absent without leave ashore. On one occasion he was brought back to the ship in Mombasa by the police – battered and bruised, but still defiant.

We continued the voyage and finally left Mombasa northbound for Aden. The crew announced that they would be holding one of their concerts in the pig. None of the passengers would see this concert unless there was a well-known entertainer on board, and then the celebrity usually got an invite – Harold Berens, Derek

Roy and Arthur English were among those who came at different times. We officers had an open invitation.

The pig was one of the few rooms on the ship with air conditioning, but it was still pretty stuffy in there when the show started with about sixty people crammed into the seats. The Captain sat in the front row with other senior officers and the performance started. As usual it was of a very high standard, and the stewards in particular made a real go of it. There was plenty of singing and dancing, and slightly dirty humour. A bunch of crewmen were doing a skit on ballet (and very funny it was!) when suddenly with a manic laugh a figure appeared hanging from a rope tied to the deckhead and swung out over the audience. He was dressed in a tutu and wore rugby boots and socks. In his hand was a fairy wand, which was waved in the Captain's face as he passed. The whooping laugh became louder with each swing, and we all suddenly realized it was Wee Georgie. He was well drunk.

Everybody was now helpless with laughter and Georgie caught on. A can of beer now appeared in his hand. He grinned down madly at the Captain.

"How's this for a few days' pay, Jimmy?" he chortled at the senior officers beneath him, and he promptly urinated in a steady stream over the old man's face.

There was then a rush by all hands to get him down, but he evaded all capture. He spun around above the outstretched hands, beside himself with glee.

The bosun appeared, and with a sharp knife he cut the drunken Scotsman down. Wee Georgie was removed, and I didn't see him again until he paid off the ship in London looking very bedraggled and sorry for himself.

His story, though, does not end there. Two years later I was one of the second officers on a big mail ship running from Southampton to South Africa – five-week round trips with ten days' leave between, ideal for the married men. The life was one of routine. Someone made up a circular calendar, and from it you could tell where each of the five big passenger vessels were at any one time, and when they would pass one another.

A group of the stewards had a standing order in the radio room every voyage to be logged in to do the football pools. One of them would come up a day after the ship sailed and hand over the money for about a dozen of them in the syndicate to the second radio officer.

Unbeknown to me, Wee Georgie was on board, working. He even had a company contract, and to a certain extent he had sobered up a bit. He was hidden down in the bowels of the ship – in the galley and working alleyway – where he was just a number, unseen by most of us. Therefore it was some surprise when, one morning after sailing while the radio officer and I were chatting in the radio room, from below the half-door of the serving hatch a Glaswegian voice enquired, "Hey, youse, ye Sassenach bastards!"

I looked over and there was Wee Georgie. He was no more than five feet high. He was barely sober.

"What can I do for you, Georgie?" the sparky asked.

"I wanna do the poo'. Here's me money," said the wee man, handing over a wodge of notes.

"What about the others?"

"They want oot, but I want in, so take it."

"OK, if that's what you want," the sparky replied, and Georgie was in the football pools.

A couple of weeks went by, and we had steamed down the West African coast and stopped off in Cape Town. Now we were making our way up the coast of South Africa. When I arrived on the bridge at midnight somewhere off Mossel Bay, the ratings in my watch looked much the worse for wear, and from down on the forward well deck the raucous sound of merriment and laughter rose up and over the bridge front.

"What's going on?" I asked Davy, the other second mate.

"Oh, that bloody Georgie has won £96,000 on the pools. All four masters-at-arms and the bosun and the watch are down there now trying to restore order."

Well, it was nearly four o'clock in the morning before calm

was achieved. Wee Georgie, insensible with drink, had planted the staff commander firmly on the chin. The logbook loomed again.

At ten thirty the next morning we deck officers, and the purserette typist were all gathered in the Captain's cabin to witness the logging and punishment of one George Woods, steward. He appeared in the doorway, hanging between two burly able seamen. He was covered in blood and vomit, and his shirt was split down his back.

"Stand up straight," ordered the Captain. "For striking a senior officer, I fine you two days' pay, and for being drunk and incapable of turning to, a further two days' pay."

"See youse, Cap'n. Double it. Up yours!" Georgie spat the words out through broken teeth.

"Another two days!" The Captain was getting mad now.

"Double it again, ye bastard."

Georgie broke free from the able seamen and started to dance around the cabin, singing, "Too-ru-roola-ro, who the bloody hell are you?"

Sighting the purserette making notes, he grasped her and plunked a blood-and-vomit kiss on her cheek. The two sailors lunged for the drunken steward.

"Leave him," said the Captain. "Here, Georgie, drink this." He handed Georgie a shot of whisky.

"Cheers, Cap'n! You're a good yin."

He swallowed the Scotch in one go and promptly collapsed insensible on the carpet. The able seamen removed the carcase and he was confined in the isolation ward on the stern of the ship, with a twenty-four-hour guard for his own safety. Wee Georgie was transferred to another ship in Durban and sent home DBS (distressed British seaman). He was certainly distressed all right.

We heard a year or so later that most of the money was gone on drink and horses, or given to or taken by his so-called friends. Ninety-six thousand pounds in 1965 was a *lot* of money.

Whatever his faults, Wee Georgie certainly livened things up for a while – an incorrigible rogue.

TILLY LING

Tilly Ling came on board in Genoa. She was tall and striking, but with a haughty air, and, as we were to find out, she was an insufferable snob. She had been a stewardess with an Australian airline and chief purser, no less, we were informed, and now she was married to our Captain. She never ceased to let us know who she was and what she was.

She took an instant liking to the second officer, a smooth individual who in better circles would be called a lounge lizard. She thought, quite wrongly, that he was better bred and educated than the rest of us. He liked to call himself a 'dog of war', having served briefly in the Sultan of Oman's navy, fighting rebels in that country. The nearest he came to action was when the only gun on board went off by mistake.

We sailed from Genoa straight out into heavy weather. In wintertime that part of the Mediterranean was notoriously rough, and on this passage it was exceptionally so. The ship heaved and rolled and heavy seas thundered over the decks. Tilly Ling retired to her bunk, much to the relief of the officers at mealtimes, as her conversation at table was either insufferable or boring. She also had a habit of rattling her knife against a glass when she wanted the attention of the steward. One day some wag in the officers' bar said, "Tilly Ling was at it again today at lunchtime," and the name stuck.

The ship passed through the Suez Canal and into much warmer weather. Tilly Ling started to appear on deck, but she never let any of us gaze on her attractive body. She took to lying in a sheltered part of the bridge deck, away from lustful eyes.

Eventually we arrived off the port of Kuwait, where we were to anchor for two weeks, we were told. My God, a long boring wait confronted us!

The Captain approached me: "When would be a suitable time for my wife to use the swimming pool?"

I knew what he was getting at, but I advised him that mid afternoon should be just right, as it was generally quiet about the ship at that time.

However, word somehow got out that Tilly Ling would be going swimming, and several officers hid up in one of the deck cranes, peering through the gaps in the steelwork. Tilly duly appeared in a large bathrobe, although it was almost 100 in the shade. Approaching the pool, she looked around and demurely let the robe slip down, revealing quite a voluptuous figure. Then she slipped into the pool and swam up to one end and back again. It was then that she saw the small shark the crew had caught and put in the pool. Letting out a scream, she set off at full overdrive speed towards the other end, but before she got there she realized there was no ladder at that end. With legs and arms flailing, she somehow made it back again to the ladder and got out. The lads in the crane were helpless with laughter.

I returned to my cabin and sat in my armchair to await the Captain. I didn't have long to wait.

"Who put that shark in the swimming pool?" he demanded.

"What shark?" I lied.

We went up on to the boat deck – the shark was gone.

Now there's a thing!

WILLY WAGTAIL

By the time the 1980s came around nearly all the famous British shipping companies had gone. Many of the ships were sold for scrap, or to Greek or Far Eastern owners for some limited trading. The cargo ships especially would not last long. They were too expensive to run and container ships were on the seas and taking all the trade. But some countries were keen to prove their nationhood, and one way was to have a merchant fleet of their own. This was particularly so with states in the Persian Gulf. The oil industry was booming, and the infrastructure of many of the Arab countries required massive investment. I therefore found myself working for a new Arab shipping company trading worldwide and into the Persian Gulf ports. Most of the ships were large with plenty of cranes and heavy derricks, and wide hatches suitable for carrying containers.

The runs were varied, from all ports in the United States, the Far East and, of course, Europe. The pay and leave were excellent and the ships well managed.

Then the Iran–Iraq War broke out. It now became extremely dicey sailing into the Gulf. Ships were stopped and detained by the Iranians and taken into port for investigation, and strange aircraft flew up and down the Gulf firing off Exocet missiles at shipping. Many ships were hit, mainly in the aft end, as the missiles always appeared to go for the steering gear.

There was no naval protection, and no convoy system; getting up the Gulf as far as Kuwait was an achievement. Many ships were hit and some sunk; several British officers were killed and injured. It never really made the news at home as British interests were not affected. It was only after several years of warfare that the Western powers started to introduce warships and carrier groups into the area to protect the vital oil route through the Strait of Hormuz.

The Iranians always appeared to have very accurate information on the cargoes coming into the area. On one occasion the ship I was on had Sidewinder missiles in containers on deck. They had come from Baltimore, destined for Abu Dhabi. At Yanbu in Saudi Arabia, on the Red Sea, the ship was detained for nearly two weeks, surrounded by troops and police. We were not allowed ashore, but it became obvious that the Saudis were aware that the Iranians knew the missiles were on their way. They took the ship out of circulation for a while. We eventually arrived safely at Abu Dhabi. There are an awful lot of people from Iran living and working in the United States, and no doubt spies were at work in ports in Japan and Korea. Very large amounts of military cargo were shipped from Brazil, and it was quite common to have at least thirty class 1 containers full of explosives on deck, with military vehicles below deck, all eventually going through from either Kuwait or Jordan to Iraq. At that time Saddam Hussein was an ally of the Western powers and had to be supported.

Brazil and the United States were not the only countries supplying Iraq with war material. The French were their biggest supplier, but they also sent munitions to Iran – especially Exocet missiles. The British also were in on the deal.

Coming down the Channel on one voyage we suddenly received orders to proceed immediately to Chapman's Creek. The charts had to be searched pretty hard before we found it, and then we had to steam well down the Channel before we could turn and come back up the route to this obscure place in the south-east of England. We then came under the direction of the Ministry of Defence and over the next two days loaded almost 300 tons of mortar bombs, rockets and machine guns, all bound for Jordan, but we knew they would then go on through to Iraq.

On one of these military voyages from Brazil, I was given coded secret orders to proceed to a position in the Red Sea and await instructions. This we did, drifting for almost three days. A message was then received to proceed to an area twenty miles off the coast of Saudi Arabia and wait again. Sure enough, a pilot launch was seen approaching and a British pilot came on board, and we steamed towards the land.

Suddenly, ahead of us a line of racon buoys lit up on the radar screen, activated by satellite. The ship then berthed at a wooden jetty in the desert and the cargo was whipped off in no time and loaded on to lorries, which then set off across the desert towards Iraq. The jetty we went to is not marked on any chart; neither are the racon buoys in the approach channel.

The pilot, incidentally, had served his time in the Clan Line. We were both now working for people we did not really trust, but they paid our wages and kept the wolf from the door.

On another occasion, approaching the Strait of Hormuz, we had steamed in close to the Oman coast to overhaul the heavy lift derrick before discharging our cargo from Japan in Gulf ports. Over the horizon a large warship was steaming directly towards us, and it circled in a few hundred yards off our stern. The ship was Iranian, and we were ordered to follow her through the strait to the port of Bandar Abbas, just inside the entrance to the Gulf in Iran.

Naval officers came on board – they were all British-trained at Dartmouth, and were quite pleasant – but some very nasty-looking men with them brandished machine guns at us all. They wanted to see all the ship's documents and informed us we were an Iraqi ship, which we were not; we flew the flag of Kuwait. Some years previously she had been under Iraqi ownership, but the flag had been changed. The original certificates were then shown to me. Now, how the hell had they got those, as they were all lodged in the head office in Kuwait? If proof was needed that you couldn't even trust your own in the Gulf, this was it.

The holds were searched, and, using our own crew, cargo was discharged on to the quayside. They could not find any military items, but the chief engineer and I were worried that they might suspect that computer parts for motor cars could be used in military vehicles.

The ship was held for almost two weeks. The naval officers told me that we were lucky the revolutionary guards were not called in; then life would have become very unpleasant for us. Pressure was put on us to take the ship further up the Gulf to another Iranian port, from where we would be flown home. We all refused that offer on a tip-off from one of the Iranian sub lieutenants. He told us that no such thing would happen and that instead the revolutionary guards would be in charge of us.

When it was realized that we would not agree to their demands, the ship was suddenly released. Our moorings were cast off and we were dumped outside the harbour. As we hurriedly steamed away across the Gulf two jet aircraft attacked us with missiles. They all missed, except for one that struck the funnel but did not explode. The aircraft had no visible national markings on them.

A day later we arrived safely off Dubai port.

A very dapper Englishman came on board and offered us an electronic system which would deflect Exocet missiles – in fact, any type of missile, he said. The gadget consisted of a large black box and a maze of wires and terminal boxes.

"Just plonk it on the fo'c's'le," he advised. "No missile will come near you – guaranteed." He infused confidence into his sales pitch.

"Fine," I said. "Looks good to me. You come with us to Kuwait and show us how it works."

He looked a little flustered. "I shall have to get in touch with my Paris office." Sweat was starting to form on his top lip.

We did not see him or his magic box again.

This situation in the Gulf continued for a considerable amount of time, and British officers received little or no support from

Foreign Office officials in Gulf ports. We worked for foreign nationals and were no concern of theirs. There was no British Embassy in Iran, and any problem there was handled by the Swedish Embassy. One ship with ten British officers on her was detained for over ten months.

Nevertheless trade to the Gulf ports continued, with the ships fully laden with all kinds of cargoes. Industrial goods, electrical items from the Far East, and even complete airport facilities were all loaded in one ship. Control towers, terminals and hangars made a complete cargo.

In the early days of Arab merchant-shipping expansion, much of the shoreside operations was run by Palestinians, brought in by the Arabs in their support of the PLO. The love affair did not last long, and after a few years the Palestinians were sent packing. Quite possibly they were seen as a threat to the United Arab Emirates and other Arab countries. Although support was still given to the PLO, many of the Gulf States banned Palestinian officers from going ashore.

Meanwhile the war between Iraq and Iran rumbled on. The Iranians lost thousands of men in infantry attacks on Iraqi positions, and it was said the carnage was greater than on the Western Front in the First World War.

I was at home enjoying a nice long leave from all this turmoil and world upheaval when I received a phone call asking me to volunteer to go into Iraq and stand by some of the company ships stranded up the Shatt-al-Arab. I would be paid 100% on my wages, tax-free. The tour of duty would last for about four months. Insurance had been paid out on 70% of the vessels' commercial value, and they were all up for sale if buyers could be found.

After talking it over with my wife and being assured by Head Office that there was little or no danger involved, I agreed to go. The old adage 'Never volunteer for anything' was later proved to be very, very wise.

Four of us flew out to Kuwait. We got off to a bad start as the agent did not turn up at the airport, and we waited nearly twenty-fours hours for him to show up. When he did, he told us it was our fault for not being in the right place the night before. He bundled us all into a large company estate car and drove out across Kuwait City. Eventually we arrived at a small hotel miles from town, and there we waited for nearly three weeks whilst our passports were processed by the Iraqi authorities.

The temperature in the shade was over 40 degrees. When a washing machine was used, the clothing was dry before you got it up on the roof to the clothes lines. Basically we were prisoners. There was very little where we were – no shops, no phones – but there was a football stadium, and at weekends there was quite a crowd of Arabs in there watching local teams. They were all very friendly to us, and kept shouting, "Bobby Charlton!" It seemed everybody knew Bobby.

Mercifully the food in the hotel was pretty good. We ate a lot of Kuwait prawns, cooked in garlic by the Korean cook, but it became very trying waiting for something to happen. At last the agent turned up and loaded us up into his car, and we set off for the border post between Kuwait and Iraq. The road from Kuwait to Safwan was busy – very busy. There may have been a war going on, but everybody was eager to make money out of the situation. Container lorries nudged along nose to tail, and cars loaded to the roof racks with televisions, fridges and food of all kinds clogged the roads and the car parks at Safwan, the border post.

It was here that I saw men known as 'drummers' – smartly dressed Arabs in gaudy suits, wearing large buttonholes, and plenty of gold rings and bracelets flashing in the sun. One dapper-looking chap was dressed in a pink suit and white winkle-picker shoes. He flashed a gold-toothed smile at us as we passed. Wars attract this type of person. The American Civil War was famous for them, and so were the Napoleonic Wars. They make their living out of the misfortune of others: buying and selling, corrupt deals, and passing information, quite often to both sides.

After several hours going through customs at Safwan, we

continued on into Iraq to the town of Basra. Military vehicles and soldiers were everywhere, all in a great hurry. They looked terribly efficient. Many of them were large, imposing men with bristling military moustaches, but many years later, up against real soldiers of the Western Alliance, they proved not to be so.

Basra was extremely hot, dirty and smelly. Many of the buildings had been hit by shellfire, and garbage and sewerage lay about in the streets. We arrived at the Hamdan Hotel in the centre of town (two stars, maybe, but it was air-conditioned). We were to stay there about a week.

That night the shelling started. The Iranians were trying to hit the port itself. We went up on the roof to watch. The gun flashes lit up the sky, but the shells appeared to be landing well short of the opposite bank of the Shatt-al-Arab, away from the docks. The firing went on all night, and flares made the horizon towards Iran as bright as day. The streets of Basra were alive with people, and there were several bars doing a roaring trade keeping the army happy with plenty of drink and girls. Some of the girls were incredibly beautiful, and many of them came from countries in Eastern Europe – a time-honoured profession that has seen countless wars over the years. The excitement of the place with the front lines so close was exhilarating.

I awoke early in the morning to the sound of noises coming from the alley outside my window. The wall of the hotel and the building opposite were alive with rats, scrabbling and squeaking. They made the most unholy din, but as the sun came up they all ran off into the drains and crevices in the brickwork.

Our stay in the Hamdan Hotel was enlivened by visits to the Basra Hilton, a large modern building down near the river. Journalists and diplomats from all over the world were staying there and trying to get stories on the war. We became very friendly with some people from the BBC, who were most interested in our movements in the country. They told us how everybody was making money from the war. Embassy officials in Kuwait would drive a car across the border and sell it in Iraq, making a huge profit on the deal and the exchange rates.

"Does our embassy do that?" I asked.

"What do you think?" they replied. "We're British."

At last we were packed up into a large estate car by an Arab gentleman. He informed us that he was called Abu Saud, and that he was our personal agent and assistant down in Umm Qasr, the port we were going to, not far from Safwan.

The drive through the desert took about an hour, and was actually not far from Safwan. The customs officer at the dock gate took a fancy to my Bausch & Lomb binoculars and confiscated them. I demanded a receipt. He very reluctantly gave me one. This was to prove almost disastrous later on.

We finally got on board the ship, which was anchored in the stream, and met the officers we had come to relieve.

Anchor watches were being kept, and if the ship got too close to the bank as the tide turned, the engines would be started and a kick ahead or astern would swing her clear. It was always hoped this operation did not happen in the early hours of the night, but sometimes, much to the annoyance of the engineer on duty, it did. When we British officers finally left the ship, the Arab replacements did not bother and she often was left stranded in the mud with her rudder and screw buried deep in the mire.

The social life on board was sparse. There was local TV to watch, and we knew when the screen went fuzzy that a shamal was approaching. The bond had long ago been drunk dry, but there was some beer, and attempts were made to brew our own and also make wine.

Once a week Abu Saud would take two or three of us up into Basra to shop and try to purchase essentials. These trips proved most exciting. We trawled the markets looking for items on the chief steward's list. The army people were everywhere, and they had first choice of virtually everything. The smell, the flies and the piles of garbage in the markets at first put us off, but we soon realized that if we were to get anything we had to put up with it. There were large numbers of Russians who were also shopping.

They were apparently helping Saddam in his war effort. Prices of foodstuffs were ridiculous. A large bag of onions would go for over £25.

I had to go once a month to the agent's office to draw Iraqi dinars. Abu Saud priced himself at about £1,000 a month equivalent. Leaving the office I would be wandering the streets of Basra with several thousand dinars in a holdall.

Once the shopping was complete, Abu Saud would take us to a restaurant for lunch. This place was run by his brother, so he said.

The lunch was always curry and rice – and very good it was too – but the main thing was that we were allowed to purchase four bottles of the local beer each. This stuff was powerful – so powerful that the trip back to the ship afterwards went by unnoticed. There were liquor stores in town selling mainly whisky and Drambuie, and a few bottles of these were carted back on board too. Our last stop before returning was the ice-cream shop. Still trading, with the shells falling all around, the owner would sit cross-legged on the table and pour bags of powder into the machinery as it whirled around. The ice cream was lovely – all different colours – and somehow we always managed to get it back on board without it melting, even though we were full of Arab beer.

The sparsity of the diet and the tension of being close to the front took its toll. We all steadily lost weight. At night the sky would be lit up by the flashes from the guns and the flares going up continuously. It was said that the white flashes were the Iraqi guns firing east, and red flashes were a sign Iranian shells were coming our way. Shells landed regularly in the desert about half a mile away, so we assumed we were just beyond the range of the enemy.

Close to the ship, perched on a hilltop, was a battery of large long-range artillery. One of these guns we nicknamed Big Bertha. At least once a week these guns burst into life, the noise becoming deafening. They were firing directly across our bow, and the shells could be seen in flight heading towards the Shatt-al-Arab several miles away to the east. I found this experience fascinating, but several of the lads found it difficult to cope with.

One morning a strange jet aircraft flew low over the ship. It had no markings on it, and smoke was coming out of the engine at the rear. It zoomed down and skidded across the desert on its belly in a cloud of sand and dust. The pilot could then be seen trying to open the cockpit cover, but he was not moving it. His movements gradually got weaker and we reckoned he must have been wounded. For three days he sat there, with nobody going near him. Occasionally we could see his arm moving, but that was all. On the third day an army truck full of soldiers drove out across the desert, shots were heard, and then the soldiers pulled the man from the aircraft. We never knew if the pilot was an Iraqi or an Iranian. He was dead, though, for sure.

One morning the guns were particularly busy. The noise got louder and louder, and the air was full of dust from the cannonades. While I was on the bridge wing watching this performance, a small bird came swooping towards the ship and landed exhausted next to me. He was a wagtail. I picked him up and carried him inside. He just lay motionless, obviously scared witless. After a while he drank some water, and we found some rice grains for him. He flatly refused to leave the wheelhouse, and he made the flag locker in the corner his home, nestling down amongst the flags and twittering away to himself. We called him Willy. He lived with us for almost three months, and became quite domesticated. His favourite drink was a dash of Drambuie, which would knock him out. He would sleep the sleep of the just, with no thoughts of war.

There was always a possibility that Iranian soldiers would come across from the direction of the port of Faw and try to get on board, so during one of our shopping trips two geese were bought, and they were given the run of the foredeck. The idea was that they would warn us of any approaching danger. They were named George and Mildred. Actually they became so possessive that it was almost impossible to pass them. Later, after we had all gone, the Arabs put them in the cooking pot.

And so we existed, with the war going on not ten miles away, and the excitement of trips into town, and endless games of bridge in the saloon. I found the situation invigorating. I felt safe from the war, but I was looking forward to getting out of Iraq and going back to Kuwait and home. Winter was now in full swing. The desert was a sea of mud, and on occasions snow and hail would fall, but never settle.

Although the war never stopped, that part of the Shatt-al-Arab and the desert around it was a stopping place for migratory birds flying south, and many different breeds would be seen feeding in the creek around us.

Then suddenly our lives were changed and the situation became dangerous and frightening. Diesel oil was running low and 100 tons of it were ordered through the agents in Basra to run the generators. The ship's engines when used also ran on diesel, whereas at sea they would have run on heavy oil.

A bunker coaster eventually arrived. It could not have come down the Shatt-al-Arab from Basra as the Iranians controlled the waterway at Faw; so it either came over from Kuwait, or was hidden away somewhere in the creek that was Umm Qasr. Anyway arrive it did and started pumping oil into the ship's tanks.

A strange white boat suddenly appeared alongside, and two smartly dressed Iraqis came on board and said that six of us were required at Immigration in town over a small matter. Four engineers and the electrician left like sheep to the slaughter, completely unsuspecting. We persuaded these men that a further engineer was required to finish the bunkers. They said they would come back for him later, but mercifully they never did. Little did we realize that they were now in the hands of Saddam's secret police.

In Basra they were put into an empty old lavatory and told to wait. They waited three days without food (there was some water), bedding or warm clothing.

Back on the ship we became increasingly concerned when they did not come back. I got Abu Saud to take me into Basra to the agent. He was reluctant to do this, but a few hundred more dinars persuaded him.

Arriving at the office, I immediately noticed about four hatchet-faced men sitting around against the walls. The agent, normally a cheerful chappie, was pale and frightened and would tell me nothing. He knew nothing, he said, and did not know where my people were. I asked him if I could phone Head Office in Kuwait, but he said the lines were down.

Eventually I got Abu Saud to take me to his brother's place for some food. The waiters in this place appeared sullen and frightened, and when I went to the toilet one of them whispered that the state police had my people.

Back on the ship, there were now only four of us left to run it, which was no problem really. I could now see that Abu Saud was an informer for the police.

It would be three weeks before the officers were returned on board. They were taken to Baghdad and put in a high-security jail. There were forty prisoners to one room, and a hole in the centre served as a toilet. At night they could hear men being tortured. They themselves were taken along for interrogation, and the torture equipment was on the table in front of them. There were no windows in the cell, but there was a hole in the roof so they could tell day from night.

One morning they were taken out and asked to line up with their hands on the shoulder of the man in front. They were then blindfolded. They were marched along for about ten minutes, seriously thinking they were going to be shot. They ended up in a garage on a main road, with cars going up and down outside. They sat there for several hours and were then bundled into the back of an army truck, which drove off at high speed. An hour or two later it pulled up sharp and they were ordered out. The truck drove off, and there in front of them was an iron fence and a white woman in a garden picking flowers. They were outside the British Consulate. They were taken in, fed, cleaned up and given warm beds to sleep in.

"Just put us on a plane to London," they asked. "As we are – in shorts and sandals."

The consul then explained that as they had come into Iraq into a military area, they would have to go out again from there. He wrote passes for them and a driver took them back to Basra. It would be another week before they got back on board. Passing through military checkpoints every few miles, they were harassed by the soldiers. By the time they eventually returned to Umm Qasr some of them were in a serious state of shock and fright.

Meanwhile back in Basra the second mate, a Punjabi, and I decided something had to be done, so we arranged for Abu Saud to take us into town to do some essential shopping. At lunchtime I engaged Abu Saud in a long discussion about football, and the second mate excused himself to go to the toilet. He climbed out of the window and got into the shop next door and asked if he could use the telephone.

"Of course, my friend," said the shop owner: "5 dinars, please."

Luckily the second mate had some money. He phoned the Kuwait office, and after a considerable delay he got through to the personnel people and told them what was going on. He was told to bring me to the agent's office the next day, where someone from Kuwait would be coming to see us.

Abu Saud was not pleased that he had to take us again the next day, but I did not tell him why – only that I had important business in Basra. So it was that the following day at lunchtime I arrived at the town office. The same hatchet-faced men were sitting around the walls, and the agent himself was pale and shaking.

A car drew up outside and an Iraqi came into the room and announced that he was the company's engineer superintendent. He demanded to know where the missing officers were.

"I was born in Basra," he declared. "If you cannot tell me, I shall go and see my friend the mayor."

The agent winced. "I can tell you nothing," he said in a whisper.

The superintendent, without a word to me, left, and they drove away.

An hour passed. He came back, running into the room with a face as white as a ghost.

"What's going on?" I enquired nervously.

"They have given me one hour to leave Basra, or I will be shot," he replied, and he was gone out of the door and into the car in a flash.

Abu Saud had also gone, never to be seen by me again. I turned to the agent and asked for a car to take me back to the ship.

One of the hatchet-faced men now spoke up: "You come with me."

Like a flash I was handcuffed and dragged outside to a car. I was then blindfolded and the car set off at high speed. It was not long before I was bundled out again and stood in the hot sun. I could hear troops marching about and a lot of shouting going on. The blindfold was suddenly whipped off and I found I was standing on a parade ground. From the look of the buildings around me it was an old army barracks. About 50 yards in front of me was a long wall with a wooden gate in it. The gate opened and three handcuffed Arabs were pushed through it by gun-toting soldiers. The men were pushed up against the wall. The soldiers moved away from them, and, before I realized what was going to happen, the guns crackled and the men were knocked over by the gunfire. One of the soldiers walked over and, aiming his rifle, shot the still-squirming figures as they lay on the ground.

The hatchet-faced man appeared alongside me: "You go back to ship. You keep quiet. Otherwise for you the same."

I was not going to let the little bastard get away with it.

"You shoot me, and there will be plenty trouble back in UK over it," I replied.

He smiled, as much as to say, "Tough!"

An hour later I was back in Umm Qasr.

The next day, much to our relief, the missing men returned. They were very distressed – especially a young engineer from Liverpool. He could not stop crying, and it was obvious we had to get him out of Iraq as soon as possible. He eventually ended up in hospital at home for several months.

It now transpired that we could not leave Iraq until emergency visas had been applied for and issued. There was now another driver sent over from Kuwait to handle this. We did not see much of him as he also was extremely frightened.

It was another three weeks before at last letters of exit were issued, and we all ended up on the dockside to travel up to Safwan.

The new driver was in a frantic hurry, and with six of us piled into the car with all our baggage he tore off up the dirt road towards Safwan.

"Wait," I cried. "I must get my binoculars back."

He threw the car round in a handbrake turn and we screamed up to the dock gate. I rushed up to the custom post and presented my receipt for my glasses. The man was taken aback but took them out of a cupboard and handed them to me. I turned to go.

"Where is your pass?" said another hatchet-faced man, sitting in the corner.

I almost fainted. "I have a letter in the car," I explained.

"No good," said he. "You must have a pass to get out of the dock."

Our car driver then appeared, mercifully waving the letters of exit in his hand.

At last the hatchet-faced man let me go. By now it was getting dark, and the driver hurled the car along the road at full speed. Suddenly ahead was a military checkpoint. A guard was sitting half asleep on a stool outside. His face dropped when he saw six Westerners sitting in the car. We had almost persuaded him that all was well when a Land Rover appeared with an officer in it.

'This is it,' I thought: 'we will never get out.'

"Where are you going?" he asked.

Like a flash and on the spur of the moment I said, "We have to get back to England to watch Manchester United in the Cup."

He waved us on.

After a further few harrowing hours on the Iraqi side of the border at Safwan the car eventually passed through into Kuwait. The relief in that car was visible – even the Kuwaiti driver was crying with relief. The second engineer then produced a bottle of whisky he had been hiding. Needless to say it did not last long.

In Kuwait we were housed in a luxury hotel, and the next day we visited Head Office, but only really got a pat on the back. We were taken round to the British Consulate and provided with food and drink. The consul was very understanding, but he became upset when I suggested that he must have known British people were missing in Iraq; the Kuwait office knew, and there were plenty of UK nationals working there who must have tipped him off. He suddenly became very political, and shortly afterwards the interview was at an end.

The very poorly young Liverpool lad was flown out that night and we never saw him again. The rest of us had to wait another week before at last we climbed aboard the Golden Budgy and flew home.

So why were our people taken? It was said we were spies for Syria, which was ridiculous. My theory was that Iraq was trying to put some form of pressure on the British Government, but it went wrong as nobody at home knew we had gone adrift. My wife did not know until I phoned her from Kuwait.

I also think the Iraqi authorities intercepted some of my mail home, which was not censored in any way. We shall never know for sure. What at first was an exciting adventure turned out in the end to be something of a nightmare.

As for Willy, I hope he lived a bit longer. He was still in the flag locker when we left, but I doubt if our reliefs took much notice of him.

Over fifteen years later I was in Tacoma and berthed astern of us was the same Arab ship. How they ever got her back to sea and operational was a mystery, as up in the desert she was falling apart. But there she was!

I did not go on board.

MON CAPITAINE

In the halcyon days of British shipping an officer could expect to wait anything up to twenty years before being promoted to master, in most cases having held a licence to command a ship for at least ten years. Generally it was a matter of 'dead men's shoes' before promotion occurred.

The majority of captains were good at their job and survived until retirement, but there were many who were just not up to it. Some were complete and utter tyrants; they made the lives of their officers and crews intolerable.

A Scottish captain I knew was so objectionable that a third officer would only last one voyage with him, if he was lucky. This man liked to be known as a hard man. He was big and bluff, and he intimidated all around him, so there was no real pleasure sailing on a voyage with him. After he retired it was said he regretted the way he had treated people, but it was a bit late by then.

Another captain would not go anywhere near the land unless he had to. He would sail 100 miles off Cape Finisterre approaching Europe, and in foggy weather he would drift for days until the visibility improved and he could proceed up the Channel. On the other hand there were others, known as 'rock-hoppers', who would steam as close as they could to any piece of land, sometimes so close inshore that it was possible to read the names above the shops along the beach front. One such unfortunate, although a senior master to his owners, took his ship so close inshore to Socotra that he ran his ship on to a rock. It was more by luck than good management that the cargo was salvaged; the ship was a total loss. This was despite warnings on the charts that Socotra should not be approached nearer than 40 miles.

Other captains were quite incapable of commanding a ship, so they took to drink – not just in small quantities. Some were drunk for days on end. This put enormous pressure on the chief officers, who found it difficult to know whether to relieve the captain of his command or go along with it and hope for the best. They usually got very little support from the management ashore on this thorny problem. Head Office knew full well what many of their captains were like, but they took very little action over the situation, preferring to let the old-boy network prevail. I sailed as mate with one captain who was a closet drinker, and he would go on a bender in dangerous waters like the English Channel or in thick fog off the South African coast. On one occasion he had been drinking whilst the ship was at anchor off East London waiting to berth, and the ship suddenly received orders to up-anchor and approach the pilot station. This captain then proceeded to drive the ship all over the anchorage at full speed, charging directly at other ships and turning away at the last minute. The crews of these vessels turned out and observed us endangering them all. I was on the fo'c's'le and was torn between leaving my post and going on the bridge or staying where I was in case of a collision. The pilot eventually got on board and the ship was berthed. Our antics had been watched by the signal station, and their report was coupled with complaints from some half-dozen ships in the anchorage. The Captain was replaced when we arrived in Durban two days later. I received a rocket from the local marine superintendent for not doing more to report his behaviour.

At that time excessive drinking was all too common amongst officers and crews. It was said that the average consumption in the bars on British ships was six pints of lager per man per day. There was a serious shortage of officers and men who wanted to go to sea, and the shipping companies made sure that life on board was similar to that ashore. Ships' bars made such big profits that on the South African coast, for instance, the bar was able to hold free functions in all ports, not once but two or three times. The local breweries would put on board their own lagers and beers and also a plentiful supply of ice in cool boxes for the celebrations.

On most ships the consumption of alcohol was well regulated, but such was the way of life at that time that the ready availability of hard liquor made most voyages a worrying experience for the more responsible officers. And of course the excessive drinking eventually caused serious health problems.

The shipping lines encouraged this so-called 'social' behaviour, and I always felt relief when being appointed to a ship with a master whom I knew to be responsible in his drinking. Joining one ship, I was told by the marine superintendent that the Captain was 'a responsible piss artist'. How wrong that description turned out to be!

I also sailed with captains who were basically incompetent. They lacked the nous to be good seamen, and some of them could not control the officers and crews under them. These people relied completely on their officers to navigate and run the ships. When all the British ships had virtually gone from the oceans, and the jobs with them, these men found it impossible to hold on to employment elsewhere. This also applied to all the drinking men, for, as shipping changed, drink on board ships became scarce or was banned altogether.

As a young navigating officer I was appointed to a large passenger vessel sailing to South Africa with immigrants to that country. I joined in the afternoon and she sailed early the next morning for Flushing to pick up more people going out to the Cape.

I was on the twelve-to-four watch and at one in the morning, approaching the Dover Strait, we ran into fog. Repeated calls to the master failed to get him up and on to the bridge. The fourth mate was dispatched to try to wake him up – again with no result. Visibility was now down to a few yards, and a major alteration of course was coming up – a situation where it was imperative that the master should be on the bridge. In desperation I called the staff commander (basically the ship's second in command). He eventually appeared, none too pleased. I found he was unable to offer any proper seamanlike advice. I think both these men thought the diversion to Flushing was something they did not have to worry about.

At the end of my watch I made a note in the logbook that the master had been called to the bridge in fog conditions and failed to arrive. The Captain had never seen me before, or sailed with me before, and on the ship's return to Southampton the Marine Superintendent asked me to remove the notification from the logbook. I refused, and I was later transferred to another passenger vessel sailing to East Africa. A few years later I again sailed with the same captain, and he was still just as useless – generally fuddled with drink.

After I had sailed as master for years on dry ships, and with non-drinking personnel, I found employment on a ship with only British officers and it was quite a cultural shock to have the problem of drink on board come to my attention again. Shipping had changed so much, and regulations were now so different, that this change took some getting used to.

So what was it like being in command of an ocean-going vessel? For the first few years the weight of the responsibility and the constant worry of all aspects of running the vessel preys on your mind, but gradually, as you become more experienced and confident, you suddenly find yourself enjoying it all, until at last the people ashore start referring to you as one of their 'senior masters'. Of course there were plenty of excitements along the way, like being broken down in the middle of the Pacific while the engineers tried to replace a cylinder liner, drifting for a week or more whilst they wrestled with the 8-ton cylinder. Eventually the faulty unit was hung off and we sailed along on three legs –

or with three engine units working. On another occasion, coming out of Coos Bay, Oregon, as we were going over the bar in a heavy swell the fog suddenly came down and at the same time the gyrocompass fell over and the helmsman could not see the magnetic compass – a problem I had been reporting for well over a year. The ship had turned to starboard to drop the pilot, and we literally struggled out to sea and away from land by sighting a star and keeping it ahead. Then we put one of the lifeboat compasses at the helmsman's feet for him to steer by. A lucky night that was! It was found later that as she bumped over the swell on the bar one of the terminal leads supplying the gyro repeaters had jumped off, causing the gyrocompass to fall over.

Sailing up from Napier, New Zealand, to Tahiti, and with a long weekend coming up, the ship lost all radio communication and we were unable to contact the port of Papeete until we were about 100 miles away. One striking aspect of this incident was that for two days the ship failed to send position reports to the London office, and this was not picked up by them. I never heard if anyone in London got a rocket over it. My ship was basically lost to the world for five days.

Many such incidents over the years put stress on me as master. With the lack of properly qualified seamen and officers, the office ashore took on more of the running of their ships by introducing quality control. This involved masses of paperwork and constant surveys by a small army of surveyors and hangers-on. Governments became interested in the safety of shipping and environment control and added more paperwork to the checklists. It was quite common to arrive in a port in the middle of the night to have a small army of people troop up the gangway and 'demand' to survey the ship and all its equipment.

In Portsmouth, England, on one voyage there were eight surveyors in the ship's office demanding to see everything, also all the cargo people were wanting this, that and the other. We had eventually got everybody organized and up and running when the local government surveyor appeared, demanding the earth. I told him to tag on at the end of the queue. He was none too pleased, but he had no choice but to agree.

Later that afternoon, when they had all gone, we had to shift ship. The gangway was up and a tug was alongside when this local man appeared and demanded to go ashore as he wanted to get home for his tea. He was politely told he could go when the 'shift ship' was complete. At 2300 hours that night we sailed for Zeebrugge.

Apart from these excitements, it gave me great satisfaction to bring a ship up through the Channel in all weathers to dock on time.

One very dark night, approaching the Wandelaar Pilot Station, I was informed that there were no pilots available; so would I take the ship up to Flushing 'under blind pilotage'?

With cargo gangs booked and waiting, and a bunker barge in the offing, time was of the essence, so I readily agreed.

This pilotage proved to be professionally most satisfying, proceeding along at almost full speed in thick weather, with the pilot ashore directing the ship from buoy to buoy by radar. The bridge officers kept a ready check on the ship's position using our own radars and GPS. We arrived at Flushing tired, but satisfied with a job well done.

And so I served the latter part of my sailing days mainly in a state of complete exhaustion – especially after calling at five European ports in less than four days. Sometimes in heavy weather I would be on the bridge for days at a time manoeuvring the vessel through mountainous seas. Therefore I was quite pleased in September 1998 to finally call it a day and retire. I rang the ship's engines off in Philadelphia at 0930 hours on 21 September and caught the plane back home.

No regrets!

MAMA INNS

My story would not be complete without the tale of a pub, a village, the characters who lived and worked there, and the many hundreds of people who came and stayed at the pub in the village over a period of forty years or more. The pub was my family home during most of my life at sea – the Half Moon Hotel in the village of Sheepwash, in what those days was a very remote part of North Devon. The characters who inhabited Sheepwash and made use of the pub are now nearly all gone and the way of life at that time has also gone, washed away by modern society and of course the Grim Reaper.

In 1957 we were living in Buckland Filleigh, about 4 miles from Sheepwash. The village of Sheepwash was a place we did not go to – in fact, we hardly knew it existed. There were no road signs in those days, and the area was very rural indeed. Motor cars were a rare luxury, and there was only one bus, which went round the villages on a Wednesday to take people to the market in Holsworthy. The climate in North Devon was harsh in winter, and hot and dry in summer. Frost, snow and ice were common in the wintertime, lasting in those days for weeks at a time. The winter gales meant that all the trees, especially the oaks, were slanted away from the prevailing wind.

Father came out of the RAF in 1957 after a distinguished war career as a Battle of Britain pilot; latterly he was officer commanding 74 Tiger Squadron on Meteor Mark 8 jet fighters. This squadron was the forerunner of the Red Arrows, and on one memorable trip, returning from a Paris air show, the contraband perfume the old man had in his cockpit burst at 40,000 feet, and he exited the aircraft at Horsham St Faith airfield smelling of roses, much to the amusement of his fellow pilots and the local customs officer.

In the winter of 1958, the year I started my first trip to sea, the Half Moon Hotel in Sheepwash was purchased for a few thousand pounds, which at that time was a large sum of money. The previous landlord, a certain Billy Beale, did not like the locals and would often lock them out; the villagers would stand outside the door of the pub throwing pebbles at the windows. There was a public bar with a concrete floor, which gave my mother nightmares with all the dust stirred up by the farm labourers' hobnailed boots, and a snug bar, down a step from the public bar. The local vicar and the Doctor would drink in the snug bar with other well-heeled patrons. They were served through a small hatchway.

Beer was supplied either from bottles or from wooden kegs lying on raised trestles. These kegs required careful management to protect the ale inside, and often on hot, humid summer nights a keg would go off.

One of the favoured bottled beers in those days was a White Worthington. It was imperative to pour the contents down the side of the glass and tip the dregs away. Failure to do so could result in violent stomach eruptions.

Mother set to with full enthusiasm to make the hotel side of the business the best there was. You could say she was the original Mrs Bucket (Bouquet). Everything had to be just right, and bad behaviour of any kind was frowned upon. Her dining room, with its oak and mahogany tables and fine china and glassware, was a delight to behold. The old man, or 'Chiefy' as he was known locally (or sometimes the Wing Co), was a keen hunter and fisherman; so he developed the sporting side of the business, at the same time attempting to make a profit out of the bar and snug.

In those days a pint of beer was about 1 shilling, and a shot of spirits about 2 shillings. A farm labourer on £11 a week very rarely touched spirits, sticking to beer, but on a Friday and Saturday night some of these men would drink up to fifteen-odd pints in an evening and still turn up for work at five the next morning.

Chiefy reckoned that if he made a profit of £5 a week the pub was doing well. He resisted having a fruit machine in the bar. "It would lower the tone," said Mother. Eventually one was fitted and made such a huge profit that Mother was supplied with a dishwasher and several chest freezers on the strength of it.

A Conservative government tightened the rules on gambling in pubs and that was the end of that profitable enterprise.

Mother, or Mama Inns as she came to be called, did all the cooking and ran the hotel. The food was of an exceedingly high standard, and Mama Inns had able assistance from Freda Harris and Doris Squires. Both of them lived in the village and worked for the family for over twenty-five years. There was also Doris Harris, whose husband, Alf, was said to be the laziest farm labourer in the area (not true really).

The fishing at that time on the River Torridge was pretty good. Large salmon were caught, quite often in excess of 25 pounds. A great character called Bert Piper was employed as the gillie, and he and Chiefy had some great times on the river, catching a lot of fish. The Half Moon Hotel fishing ran for several miles downstream from above Sheepwash Bridge, with some ten-odd fishing beats along it. Pools like Peninsular and Go Lightly became household names among local fishermen.

Bert had finished the First World War in Netley Hospital near Southampton after suffering the horrors of the trenches. After returning to Sheepwash, he worked on several farms in the area and married Selena, who was ten years his senior. Eventually he called her Mrs Viper (or the Viper) because of her harsh tongue. Chiefy arranged for Bert and the Viper to

135

acquire a council house in the village after living in a tied cottage at a shilling-a-week rent for many years.

Freda asked Bert in the bar one night how he enjoyed life in a proper house with a bathroom.

Bert, then seventy, replied, "'Tis master, Freed. I even said to the missus, 'Go on, stop taking the pill and us'll give it a chance.'"

The Viper was eighty-one.

The characters who inhabited the bar were mainly local farmers and their workers, all independent in their own right, and all proper countrymen.

There was Bill Slee, who sat on the settle with one pint all night; there was Alf, who played some useful darts but very rarely won; and there was Syd Cudmore, who was useless and was married to Rene, who suffered with the big clod for years. Another Bill was the village imbecile and made everybody laugh with his antics. And then there was Ceephos.

Ceephos Piper was basically what was known in those days as a tramp. He lived in a metal hut in a village nearby and walked the two miles or so into Sheepwash for his beer. He had never washed since God knows when, and he would go round the bar picking the fag ends out of the ashtrays and rolling his own from the remains. Plonking himself down near the bar fire, he would sit and ruminate until closing time. Chiefy got fed up with him picking up fag ends, so at the end of a bar session he would tip the contents of the ashtrays into Ceephos's pot. The old boy was in fact a very intelligent man, and it was thought he had been an officer in the army but his experiences in the trenches had destroyed him. After many years, do-gooders in social services got hold of him and cleaned him up and put him into a home where he had a bed with clean sheets. He died there after six months.

A venerable local farmer would sit outside the front door of the pub with his pint, and one fine summer's day an expensive car drew up and a city gent got out and enquired of the old boy,

"Good day, my man. Have you lived here all your life?"

"No, not yet" was the reply.

The parish policemen was PC Kettle. He travelled the villages on a pushbike. Chiefy caught him late one night attempting to look through the bar windows at a party going on in the bar. Chiefy crept up behind him and PC Kettle nearly boiled over. He was invited in and he joined in the festivities, being told the revellers were all hotel guests. He left in the early hours of the morning, happy.

Another character who livened up proceedings was a newly appointed vicar, the venerable Reverend Roberts. An odd man to say the least, he had fought with a British expeditionary force for the White Russians against the Bolsheviks in 1922 and returned to England with decidedly left-wing views. He was one of the first people locally to drive a Russian car. He wandered around unshaven and with only an army greatcoat on. He started coming to the back door of the pub to buy a bottle of spirits. Chiefy got fed up with this and one night, when he called, Chiefy said to the closed door, "Hello, vicar, bottle of Morgan's, is it?"

The Reverend then got himself on to Radio Luxembourg, on a programme which was a forerunner of the modern chat shows. He complained that he had never ever seen a £5 note from the poor stipend he received from the church. Chiefy then got fed up with people calling into the bar offering money for 'your poor vicar'.

But Reverend Roberts really hit the headlines when he travelled to London and sat on a panel for *The People* newspaper. The ignorant parson thought he was going to be an adjudicator, but it turned out that *The People* was running a story about a woman who wanted a man to father the most perfect child in Britain. There was Mr Universe, who guaranteed 100% success. The wife of another candidate pulled him out of the competition when he told her it might take more than one go. Sales of the newspaper soared, especially when it became known that on the shortlist was the Reverend Roberts of Sheepwash. A large black car with a gaitered bishop turned up in the village, and that was the end of the vicar's trips to London.

The Half Moon Hotel also had a succession of well-known animals. There was Delilah, a cow who for over fifteen years supplied the hotel with milk and clotted cream; there was Yog, a poodle who would sit in the square and howl when the church bells rang; and there was Spiegel, a black tomcat. He was called Spiegel because his coat was so shiny you could see your reflection in it, and 'mirror' in German is *Spiegel*. His favourite spot was on the old wooden settle by the bar fire; and if anyone was sitting there when he came in, he would jump up on their lap, purring deliciously. After being petted for a few minutes he would sink his claws into the offender's lap, and generally regain his seat. Spiegel lived for more than seventeen years.

Another animal that made a hit was one of brother Benji's dogs, a large Labrador called Sam. Sam was oversexed, and even after suffering the final cut would still attempt to roger anything that came near him. This included humans, and as he was rather a large dog he could actually knock people over. Poor Iris Hawkins, a lady of the village, was 'rogered' unmercifully for several minutes after being felled as she walked across the square. Sam's greatest claim to fame occurred when a honeymoon couple arrived and Chiefy put them in one of the annexes across the yard behind the pub.

"Simply super!" said the young bride after dinner, as they headed off to their room.

Chiefy awoke the next morning to see the young woman in tears outside his bedroom window.

"I think we might need a doctor," she said. "My husband is seriously hurt."

Chiefy went across to the annexe to investigate. Apparently the pair were in the throes of passion when Sam got into the room and jumped on the husband's back. Keeping a straight face, Chiefy examined him and reckoned a day or two's rest would put him right.

After suffering many hard winters Mama Inns and Chiefy decided it was time to install a central-heating system. Profits were looking up a bit, so a firm in Bideford was employed one winter to do the work. At the same time Ivor Gidee, who owned a furnishing firm in Bideford, fitted the dining room out with a new carpet, which was not cheap. The work went on through the winter and at last, a few days before the hotel reopened for the start of the fishing season, on the first day of March the job was finished. All gathered in the bar for a celebration drink, the workmen making the most of the hospitality.

Mama Inns, who had been fussing about in the kitchen, decided to go into the dining room for one last check. Humming to herself she opened the door, and there hanging in a great bulge was the lath-and-plaster ceiling. As she looked at it, it collapsed, releasing hundreds of gallons of water into the room all over the tables and, of course, the carpet. Screams from Mama Inns drew the inebriates from the bar into the room. The last man in the loft space had forgotten to untie the ball cock in the header tank.

Ivor was summoned, and within twenty-fours hours the room was dried and another carpet had been laid. The hole in the ceiling was patched (sort of), and the hotel opened for business on time.

Mama Inns' annoyance with the concrete floor in the bar was solved when it became known that Annery Barton near Bideford was being renovated and the slate slabs were being taken up from a kitchen floor. Chiefy managed to purchase them for a very small sum and they were hauled over to Sheepwash by Land Rover. The slabs were large pieces of Delabole slate, and it took several trips to deliver them safely. The concrete was dug up and a mixture of sand, salt and ash put down before the slabs were laid out on the bar floor. They proved most practical. A quick wipe over in the morning removed all traces of the hobnailed-boot marks, and they also added an ambiance to the bar. Walter Raleigh stayed at Annery Barton when he was courting the 'Rose of Torridge', so maybe we all tramped where Walt put his feet. The slabs are still there to this day, fifty years on.

The Half Moon Hotel flourished. It became the centre of village life, and one of the favourite watering holes in the area – in Devon and the whole of England for that matter! The bar was the centre of attraction, and many were the parties and drinking sessions that took place there. At the children's Christmas party Chiefy got himself wedged up the bar chimney piece dressed as Father Christmas. Eventually he fell out, and a small voice piped up, "You'm not Daddy Christmas; you'm the Wing Commander."

Another Christmas night, with the bar packed seven deep, a local, Mr Punch, tried to enter the bar on his horse dressed as Father Christmas and knocked himself out on the door lintel. Then there was Farmer Sparks. He drank only Black Label Scotch – very expensive in those days – and kept Chiefy afloat with regular purchases. One night he was eventually sent off across the square, weaving crazily into the night. He was found the next morning lying in a ditch by the roadside.

"What be doin' there, Varmer?" enquired his rescuer.

"Bugger! I took the corner too fast," said the farmer.

Numerous were the occasions and numerous were the people who drank and stayed in the Half Moon Hotel – not least the many hundreds of fishermen who stayed there over the years. Some were very good fishermen, and some were not so good. Most were there for the fantastic welcome and food they received from Mama Inns and the family. Brother Benji's Bar was now famous just about everywhere. Among the more memorable guests were two Birmingham scrap dealers, short and fat with bald heads. They were nicknamed Bulganin and Krushchev, after the Russian leaders of the time. Not much fishing done by those two! Dudley Thomas and Jack Spratt were regular callers. Jack Spratt, I think it was, thought of the idea of having an end-of-fishing-season dinner in September, and all the regular residents would turn up for the event. This carried on for many years, even after Jack had passed on.

Then there was Major Jameson, whose son Christopher bought a new sports car, and coming into Sheepwash he rolled it over the hedge into Lewy Medland's field. There was much anguish after that event.

George and Gladys Marriott were regular callers, and George became more famous after he unfortunately died. He requested that his ashes be scattered into the river at his favourite fishing spot. His ashes duly arrived at the pub, and Benji put them up on the dresser in the kitchen. Mama Inns was not too happy with George sitting up there, so he was put out in the shippen with Delilah. Parson Bob Venton agreed to officiate at the scattering and Benji went out and retrieved the urn, only to find the ashes had got damp and gone solid. He placed them in the Aga to dry out, and promptly forgot them. Mama Inns came across the casket in her Aga, and the ashes inside had all gone black. Crisis! But Chiefy was up to it, and after a good stirring with some white sand George was up and running.

A large party assembled below Sheepwash Bridge for the ceremony, Chiefy with his bottle of gin and ice handy. A stiff gale was blowing. Bob Venton scattered George, who drifted down over the gathered throng. There was much spitting and coughing, and Chiefy held his hand over the glass of gin to keep George out.

All the regular guests became friends of the family, coming year after year. Their stay was not just a few days in a hotel, but a return to see the Inniss family, the pub, the village locals, and Muriel.

Chiefy would also take guests fishing from his boat *Shelduck*, which was moored at Appledore. The main sport was sea bass. Those who were paying for the trip had to do as they were told. Peter Hall disobeyed Chiefy's instructions on one occasion and was left stranded on a sandbar several hundred yards from the shore – and the tide was coming in. He did not disobey the skipper again after that.

The Sheepwash Flying Association was formed, and annual

air days were held in the airfield belonging to Charlie Trace. Benji was the air traffic controller, and John Harris, Freda's son, was issued with two white table-tennis bats to direct traffic into the car park. Several different types of light aircraft would turn up. Some of the more nervous pilots would look at the approach over the mains electric power lines and turn round and fly home. Many, though, did land. One plane with two engines, flown by an airline pilot, required a really long take-off. Unfortunately the wind shifted into the south, which meant a run downhill then up over the power lines and across the river. A hole was cut in the road hedge and the plane's tail was stuck through it to give the pilot more of a chance. With engines revving, and Chiefy, Peter Hall and me standing alongside making signs of the cross in full view of the rather pale passengers inside, the aircraft lurched away across the field, engines roaring. It managed to clear the electric cables with a few feet to spare.

As for me, I won a draw prize for a flight in one of the planes. Benji kept making announcements for me on the Tannoy, and eventually I was cornered and persuaded to get into a Fieseler Storch – a very light but safe aeroplane. The pilot got a bit miffed about my weight, and had to alter the trim quite a bit to compensate. He was also not pleased about Peter Hall and Chiefy standing outside the aircraft with hands together as if in prayer.

We flew round for ten minutes or so, and then made our approach back to the airfield, coming in now over the same power lines beyond the river. Biggles asked me to keep a close lookout behind for anything coming in astern of us. He was on his final approach when I looked round and thought I saw a speck in the sky directly astern.

"Bandits," I shouted out, "right astern."

The aircraft pulled up and went round in a tight turn, Biggles making funny noises into his mike. There was nothing there. We landed very quickly, and, after mouthing obscenities at me, the pilot informed the association committee he would not, repeat *NOT*, take any more people for flying trips.

Muriel Braunton had now joined the team behind the scenes at the Half Moon Hotel and became secretary, handling all the accounts, invoices and the now numerous load of VAT returns. Muriel became a mainstay, and her friendly smile and great cooking made her a favourite with all our guests.

Sadly Mama Inns passed away in the summer of 1975, the stress of work bringing on a brain haemorrhage. Charlie Boy now came into the operation and took over the management and running of the hotel.

This now added fresh impetus to the business, with the Half Moon Hotel staying open for most of the year. Fishing and beats on the river were improved. Charlie organized the stocking of the river each year with several hundred trout, the majority of which were caught by visiting fishermen.

Sheepwash then really went on to the map. An annual golfing cup was organized at Bude Golf Club, and it was a great honour for the golfer who won the Sheepwash Cup. This event continues to this day.

Chiefy eventually retired permanently to Barbados, leaving the running of the pub to Benji and Charlie. Handsome profits were made, most of which were ploughed back into the hotel to refurbish the rooms and the buildings.

After almost forty-five years the business was eventually sold after Chiefy had passed over the bar, but the name and the memories of the Half Moon Hotel linger on: on hot summer nights, labourers coming in late after hours working in the fields at hay harvest to enjoy the cool beer and atmosphere of the pub; on cold winter days, the warmth of the bar fire and the conversations with a fine group of friends; the darts matches; the Christmas draws; the wonderful meals in Mama Inns' dining room . . .

A way of life has now gone from the English countryside. Nothing will ever equal it.

Well done, Mama Inns!

A SUMMARY OF THE CAREER OF
J. R. DE L. INNISS

1953–7   Educated at Shebbear College, North Devon.

1954   First went to sea as a cadet boy seaman on HMS *Illustrious*.

1955   Spent two months on a small ship based in Goole called the *Rother*.

1957   Attended the School of Navigation at Warsash as a trainee deck officer.

1958–62 Sailed as a cadet on the *Clan Macbeth* of Glasgow.

1962   Gained second mate's certificate.

1962–8   Served on many different vessels, from tramps and other cargo ships to Union Castle passenger liners and a tanker, the *Scottish Ptarmigan*.

1968   Gained master's certificate foreign-going.

1968–73 Became cadet training officer for the Clan Line, and then chief officer of the SA *Vaal* on the mail run to South Africa.

1973–6   Worked ashore as assistant marine superintendent in Durban, South Africa.

1976   Joined the British & Commonwealth Shipping Company.

1980s   Served with United Arab Shipping of Kuwait.

1990   Promoted to master with Blue Star Ship Management.

1998   Retired from sea.

J. R. de L. Inniss is now chairman of his local Branch of the Royal British Legion and treasurer of the Dartmoor Dog Training and Agility Club.